SmartIcons

 Draw a macro button

 Select all objects

Increase the size of
displayed cells

Decrease the size of
displayed cells

Display cells in default
size

Show or hide parts of the
1-2-3 window

Select the data to print

Set rows as print titles

Set columns as print titles

Size data to printed page

 Select a macro
command

Turn Trace mode on or off

Turn Step mode on or off

Show or hide the
transcript window

Create a query table

Cross-tabulate values
from a database table

Find solutions that meet
constraints

Check spelling

 Size data by columns to
printed page

Size data by rows to printed
page

Insert a horizontal page
break

Insert a vertical page
break

Set orientation to portrait
mode

Set orientation to
landscape mode

Set the printed page layout

Center print range
horizontally *(New)*

Center print range
vertically *(New)*

Center Print Range both
ways *(New)*

 Send data by electronic
mail

Arrange open windows
side by side

Arrange open windows
diagonally

Go to upper-left cell

Find lower-right corner of
active area

Find next cell up adjoining
blank cell

Find next cell down
adjoining blank cell

Find next cell right
adjoining blank cell

Find next cell left adjoining
blank cell

Go to the next worksheet

 Start SmartPics

Display values with
Japanese yen

Set map redraw for this file
to automatic

Set map redraw for this file
to manual

 Play back Transcript window
contents

Make Button in transcript
(New)

Redraw all maps in this file

Draw a map *(New)*

The Official Guides to Lotus®Software

SYBEX, in conjunction with Lotus Publishing, is pleased to present the most authoritative line of books about Lotus Software you can find. The line is called *Lotus Books* and they are the ONLY guides officially endorsed by Lotus Development Corporation, the world's third largest software developer.

No matter how many features you know about a particular software package or how creative you become in using your applications, there is always something more you can learn to make your work easier and faster. That's where *Lotus Books* tutorials and references can help.

Lotus Books offer you a wealth of advantages you can't get anywhere else. First of all, *Lotus Books* tutorials and references, thanks to the reputation of SYBEX and Lotus Publishing, feature the most respected and knowledgeable authors in the computer industry. Secondly, *Lotus Books* titles, as the only official books about Lotus software, are unmatched in their accuracy and insider expertise. Finally, there are books in the *Lotus Books* family for Lotus software users of nearly every level of skill. Whether you're a beginner, an expert, or somewhere in between, you'll be able to find useful, timely and relevant information that will make your time on the computer more productive and enjoyable.

Lotus Books tutorials and references cover the full range of Lotus software applications. There are books about cc:Mail, Lotus 1-2-3, Smart-Suite, Approach and much more. You'll find *Lotus Books* wherever computer books are sold. Ask for them by name and soon you'll know the joy of learning about Lotus software from the Lotus software experts.

For a complete catalog of our publications, please write:

SYBEX Inc.
2021 Challenger Drive
Alameda, CA 94501
SYBEX Tel: (510) 523-8233/(800) 227-2346 Telex: 336311
Fax: (510) 523-2373

SYBEX is committed to using natural resources wisely to preserve and improve our environment. As a leader in the computer book publishing industry, we are aware that over 40% of America's solid waste is paper. This is why we have been printing the text of books like this one on recycled paper since 1982.

This year our use of recycled paper will result in the saving of more than 15,300 trees. We will lower air pollution effluents by 54,000 pounds, save 6,300,000 gallons of water, and reduce landfill by 2,700 cubic yards.

In choosing a SYBEX book you are not only making a choice for the best in skills and information, you are also choosing to enhance the quality of life for all of us.

1-2-3® Release 5 for Windows™ Instant Reference

Gerald E. Jones

SYBEX

San Francisco • Paris • Düsseldorf • Soest

Acquisitions Editor: Joanne Cuthbertson
Developmental Editor: Richard Mills
Editor: Michelle Nance
Technical Editor: Tanya Strub
Book Designer: Ingrid Owen
Production Artist: Ingrid Owen, Helen Bruno
Screen Graphics: Ingrid Owen
Desktop Publishing Specialist: Thomas Goudie
Proofreader/Production Coordinator: Janet Boone
Indexer: Nancy Guenther

Cover Designer and Illustrator: Joanna Gladden

Library of Congress Card Number: 94-67530
ISBN: 0-7821-1583-7

Manufactured in the United States of America
10 9 8 7 6 5 4 3

Acknowledgments

A team of dedicated professionals worked to develop and produce this book. At SYBEX, thanks to Richard Mills, Developmental Editor; Michelle Nance, Editor; and Tanya Strub, Technical Editor. Thanks also to Candace Clemens at Lotus Development Corporation for furnishing software. Special thanks are due Peter Nathan, who revised substantial portions of the first edition. And a personal thank you to Georja Oumano Jones for her wit and optimism.

Table of Contents

Introduction

Part I

What's New in Release 5?

Part II

Command and Topic Reference

Part III

@Function Reference
247

Index

Introduction

The idea governing this book is a simple one. When you are thwarted by a function or procedure in Lotus 1-2-3 for Windows, or require a quick refresher on spreadsheet techniques, you want a single source of information to solve your problems quickly. This book is intended to meet those needs.

Lotus 1-2-3 Release 5 for Windows Instant Reference provides the information essential to getting the most from this powerful version of 1-2-3. The book covers basic spreadsheet analysis and output operations, as well as functions, macros, charting, drawing, and built-in desktop publishing features. Features that will be new to users of Releases 2 and 3 for DOS and Release 1 for Windows are summarized in the section "For Experienced Users of 1-2-3," later in this introduction.

Because we expect you to consult this book as a reference for solving day-to-day application problems, we have assumed that your copy of the program is already installed. To customize the program once installation has been performed, see *Page Setup*, *Printer Setup*, *User Setup*, and *Worksheet Defaults* in Part II.

A QUICK INTRODUCTION TO 1-2-3 FOR WINDOWS

The following notes cover some of the questions commonly encountered when installing and running Lotus 1-2-3 for Windows. You must install Windows first, then 1-2-3.

To Start the Program

1. Load Microsoft Windows. At the DOS prompt, type **win**. (If you intend to work in Windows regularly, this instruction should be added to the AUTOEXEC.BAT file so that Windows loads automatically when you boot your computer.)

2. The Program Manager window will be displayed. If it is not open, select the Program Manager icon.

3. In the Program Manager window, double-click on the Lotus Applications icon or move the pointer to it with the arrow keys and press ↵.

4. In the Lotus Applications window, double-click on the 1-2-3 for Windows icon or move to it with the arrow keys and press ↵.

5. An hourglass icon will appear at the pointer location, indicating that you must wait for the program to load. The 1-2-3 for Windows application window will then appear. When the pointer changes from an hourglass to an arrow and when *READY* is displayed in the bottom-right corner of the screen, the program is ready for your input.

For more information on Windows and opening a worksheet in 1-2-3, see *New File* and *Opening a File* in Part II.

For Experienced Users of 1-2-3

If you are an experienced user of Lotus 1-2-3, you can begin using the Windows version immediately. When you see the menu bar displayed across the top of the screen, simply press the slash (/) key, just as you have always done to initiate commands. (You can also press the less-than (<) symbol.) Pressing either of these keys brings up the 1-2-3 Classic menu, which contains the commands that are familiar to you:

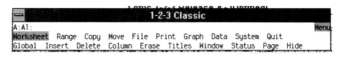

You can continue by pressing the first letter of the menu item you wish to select, then pressing the first letter of each submenu command, and finally entering any options. In short, you can use the Classic menu as you did in previous releases of 1-2-3. *Note that the command set corresponds to Lotus 1-2-3 Release 3.1 for DOS.*

Similarly, you can press the colon (:) key to work with the WYSI-WYG menu:

Keep in mind, however, that your productivity should increase and you can use much more extensive capabilities if you learn to work in the Windows environment. To do this, you need to use the 1-2-3 menu bar, the commands for which are covered in Part II.

Users of Release 4 for Windows will find descriptions of new commands and features in *Part I: What's New in Release 5?*.

LAN Installation

The 1-2-3 for Windows program can be installed on a network server if you begin with the Install disk (Disk 1 in the distribution set). Once the program has been installed on the server, installation to any node can be performed by selecting the Install 1-2-3 icon. However, you cannot install to another server by selecting this icon.

To Work in 1-2-3

Windows provides the following methods of selecting data and objects, initiating program actions, and setting options.

The Mouse

In Windows applications, menu selections are made and option settings are chosen with a pointing device, such as a mouse, trackball, or pen, and data is input mainly through the keyboard. Using the charting and drawing capabilities will be cumbersome without some type of pointing device.

Menu commands can be selected with a single-button mouse or with the left button on two- or three-button models. Use of quick menus requires a second, right button. The third, or middle button, if present, is not used.

Instructions in this book call for three types of actions with the mouse:

Click Use the mouse to move the pointer to the item described in the instruction and press the mouse button briefly, once.

Double-click Move the pointer with the mouse to the item described in the instruction and press the mouse button twice in rapid succession.

Drag Press the mouse button, hold it down while moving the pointer to the desired location, and then release the button.

Submenus

If you see an arrowhead (➤) after the name of an item in a pull-down menu, selecting that item will cause a submenu to appear. In Windows terminology, this submenu is called a *cascading menu*, or *cascade*.

If you see an ellipsis (…) after the name of an item in a pull-down menu, selecting that item will cause a *dialog box* to appear. A dialog box is a special window display in which you can change option settings.

Options   In general, options are set within dialog boxes. In Windows, different kinds of graphic symbols are used within dialog boxes to indicate the type of selection being made.

To Change Dialog Box Settings

1. When a dialog box appears, click on any button, check box, or radio button to reset or activate it. (*Or*, see *Dialog Box Keys*, below.)

2. Click on any list box or drop-down box to activate it. Drag a list to scroll it and release to select the highlighted item.

    or

    Double-click on any list item to select it.

3. Click on a text box to activate it. A flashing vertical bar appears at the insertion point. Type the text or data required.

4. If you are working in 1-2-3 and are setting an option that requires a range selection, you can click the Range Selector button in the dialog box and drag the range in the sheet.

5. Also in 1-2-3 dialog boxes, you can click the ↑ or ↓ buttons of Numeric Indicators to increase or decrease the value shown:

6. When you have finished making entries in a dialog box, click OK. (You must sometimes select Close instead.) To reset the options and return to the previous menu, click the Cancel button.

To get context-specific help in any 1-2-3 dialog box, click the ? button in its upper-right corner.

Dialog Box Keys

These are some of the keyboard shortcuts that are useful in making dialog box selections:

Alt-*letter*   Chooses the option or command with the underlined letter.

Alt-F4   Cancels the command and closes the dialog box.

Alt-Spacebar   Opens the dialog box's control menu, which contains Move and Close commands.

Alt-↑ or **Alt-↓**   Opens or closes a drop-down list box.

End   Selects the last item in a drop-down box or list box.

Enter or **↵**   Completes the command and closes the dialog box.

Esc   Closes the dialog box without completing the command (equivalent to Cancel).

Home   Selects the first item in a drop-down box or list box.

PageUp or **PageDown**   Selects the top or bottom item in a drop-down box or list box.

Shift-Tab   Moves the highlight to the previous option, from bottom to top and right to left (reverse direction of Tab).

Tab   Moves the highlight to the next option, from left to right and top to bottom.

↑ ↓ ← →   Arrow keys move the highlight within a group of options.

Windows

In the Windows environment, framed areas of the screen can represent different programs and files. A program window is called an *application*, and a file window is called a *document*. Multiple windows can be open at the same time, as when working on multiple-sheet 1-2-3 files or when doing some type of multitasking, such as editing a worksheet while printing a document with a word processing program.

Basic Features of 1-2-3

Here are some controls and features that might be different from similar operations you have learned in other Windows applications or in other versions of 1-2-3.

Context-sensitive menus and SmartIcon sets   Include the Chart, Range, and Query pull-down menus, as well as the SmartIcon sets Charting, Drawing, Query, and Transcript. The command selection appears on the menu bar, or the SmartIcon set is displayed after you have created or selected an object to which those controls would apply. For example, if you select a query table in a sheet, the Query menu item and its SmartIcon set will appear.

Drag-and-drop copying and moving   Can be done with the mouse to copy or move data without using menu commands. Select a cell or range, then move the pointer to the edge of the selection. The pointer will change to a hand symbol. Hold down the Ctrl key while you drag the selection to copy it or just drag to move it.

File operations   Import and export operations are incorporated with the File ➤ Open and File ➤ Save As commands.

@Function Selector   Clicking the @Function Selector button—located to the left of the contents box—when a cell is selected displays a list of @functions. Selecting one of them pastes its name and syntax directly into the contents box. (See Part III.)

Live status bar   Appears across the bottom of the screen and provides quick access to options such as fonts, point sizes, and toolbars.

Navigator   Clicking this button—located to the left of the contents box—displays a drop-down listing of range names. Click a range name to select it.

Quick menus   As a work shortcut, pressing the *right* mouse button when an object is selected will bring up a quick menu of commands that apply to the selected object type. Quick-menu commands activate the same dialog boxes that can be accessed through the menu bar.

Ranges   Can be selected either before or after initiating a command. Whenever the Range text box appears in a dialog box, clicking its button will activate the Range Selector pointer, which can be used to drag a selection in the sheet. (Or, a range reference, such as an address or name, can be typed into the box.) Three-dimensional ranges can also be specified by preceding a range reference with the letter or name of the sheet, followed by a colon.

SmartIcons   A row of icons normally appears across the top of the program window. You can click on an icon as a shortcut to selecting some of the commands. Consult the inside front and back covers for icons and their corresponding actions.

Worksheet tabs   Three-dimensional sheets can now be managed as though they were file folders with named index tabs. Enter the sheet name directly on its tab. Click a tab to switch to the sheet.

HOW TO USE THIS INSTANT REFERENCE

For ease of use, this Instant Reference is divided into the following sections:

Introduction

This section covers background information on Lotus 1-2-3 for Windows and gives directions for using this book.

Part I: What's New in Release 5?

Brief entries in this section summarize the commands and features that have been added or enhanced since Release 4.0.

Part II: Command and Topic Reference

Entries in this section are the names of tasks you perform in 1-2-3, rather than the names of the commands you would use to perform those tasks. If you know the name of a specific command, look it up in the Index, where you will find the page reference to the corresponding task in this section.

Part III: @Function Reference

Predefined formulas, or *@functions*, are covered in this part. Entries are arranged alphabetically within the following categories: Calendar, Database, Engineering, Financial, Information, Logical, Lookup, Mathematical, Statistical, and Text.

Endpapers

SmartIcons and their definitions are shown on the inside front and back covers of this book. (For tables of accelerator keys and function keys, see *Keyboard Shortcuts* and *Function Keys* in Part II.)

Procedures

Each entry in Part II of this book is designed to provide the information essential to understanding a particular feature of 1-2-3 for Windows in a clear, accessible format. When you need to be reminded only of the menu sequence to follow, see the entry's *To...* section.

While most actions in 1-2-3 for Windows can be handled through the keyboard, if necessary, the discussion in this book assumes that you are using a keyboard *and* a mouse. The instructions in this book refer first to the mouse actions required for menu selections and option settings with a minimum of keyboarding. However, for situations in which you might be using only the keyboard, as in data entry operations, the required keystrokes are given.

Following the Lotus 1-2-3 convention for command syntax, sequences of command selections sometimes are combined as compound commands in the text. For example, Tools ➤ User Setup ➤ International is shorthand for, "From the Tools pull-down menu, select User Setup, then select the International button in the dialog box."

Following Instruction Steps

To show at a glance the alternative paths you can follow in a single menu sequence, the instructions in this book specify the item to be selected at each step. Because the emphasis is on using the mouse to make menu selections, not all methods will necessarily be shown. A typical sequence of steps looks like the following selection.

To Set Printer Options

1.   From the File pull-down menu, select Printer Setup.

2.   In the File Printer Setup dialog box, select the printer name in the Printer list box.

3.   To accept the default options for the printer you've selected, select OK.

  or

  To change the options, select the Setup button.

4.   A dialog box containing options for the installed printer appears. Reset the options shown. (See *Options*, below.)

5.   Select OK.

Notes, Options, and Cross-References

Exceptions and possible pitfalls are described under the *Notes* headings. These sections also may include suggestions as to the most efficient work method when several alternatives are available.

The next section of longer entries is headed *Options* and usually covers any settings that can be made in submenus and dialog boxes.

Finally, where appropriate, you'll find cross-references to features of related interest under the heading *See Also*.

Part I

What's New in Release 5?

Release 5 of Lotus 1-2-3 for Windows is similar in appearance and operation to Release 4, but with a number of significant enhancements. The entries in this part of the book describe the new features since Release 4.

If you are upgrading from Release 1 for Windows, the changes will seem much more extensive to you, particularly the fact that many of the menu commands were renamed in the transition from Release 1 to Release 4. For example, the Release 1 command Worksheet ➤ Insert ➤ Column has been changed to Edit ➤ Insert ➤ Column in Releases 4 and 5.

To find the specific command required for any task, look up the descriptive name of the task in Part II of this book. For example, you would look under the entry *Inserting Cells and Worksheets* to find the procedure and options for Edit ➤ Insert ➤ Column.

Help for SmartIcons   Appears as text inside a *bubble* (resembling a speech balloon in a cartoon) when you pause the mouse pointer over a SmartIcon. The bubble will also appear if you point to a SmartIcon with the mouse and press the *right* mouse button.

As in previous releases for Windows, when you make a selection from the menu bar, a description of the command or operation will appear in the upper-left corner of the screen.

SmartIcons   **New to Release 5** are 100% Vertical Bar, 100% Horizontal Bar, Center Across Columns, Center All On A Page, Center Horizontally On A Page, Center Vertically On A Page, Create Dynamic Crosstab, Create Form, Create Mailing Labels, Create Report, Default Currency, Make Button In Transcript, Mixed Chart, Quick File New, Quick Print, Start Approach, and Start ScreenCam.

The following SmartIcons have been renamed: 3D Vertical Area Chart, 3D Vertical Area Chart With Depth, 3D Vertical Bar Chart, 3D Vertical Bar Chart With Depth, 3D Vertical Line Chart With Depth, Vertical Area Chart, Vertical HLCO Chart, Vertical Line Chart, and Vertical XY Chart Without Lines.

Top Ten Help Topics   Explains the ten most frequently executed tasks in Lotus 1-2-3 for Windows. Descriptions and procedures can be found by selecting Help ➤ Contents ➤ Top Ten Tasks. The topics include previewing and printing, file operations, @functions and formulas, styling, arranging data, charting, databases, macros, rows and columns, and templates.

In-Cell Editing   Is a new feature by which both the formula bar and the selected cell open when you are typing a keyboard entry. You can then edit the data either in the formula bar or directly in the cell. To accept the entry, click the ✓ button next to the formula bar, press ↵, or just click any other cell in the sheet.

Commands—New and Revised   Commands added or changed since Release 4 are shown in Table I.1, which also lists the topic in Part II under which the procedure for each command is presented.

Table I.1: New and revised commands since Release 4

Command	Type of Change	Reference Topic
File ➤ Doc Info	New	Document Information
File ➤ New	Revised	New File, SmartMasters
File ➤ Open	Revised	Opening a File
File ➤ Print Preview	Revised	Previewing Printouts
File ➤ Save As	Revised	Saving a File
Range ➤ Format	Revised	Currency Formatting
Range ➤ Go To	Deleted	Go To
Range ➤ Justify	Deleted	Alignment
Range ➤ Name ➤ Paste ➤ Table	Deleted	Navigator
Range ➤ Protect/ Unprotect	Deleted	Protecting Ranges and Files
Style ➤ Fast Format	New	Fast Range Formatting
Tools ➤ Database ➤ Dynamic Crosstab*	New	Cross-Tabulation
Tools ➤ Database ➤ Form*	New	Forms for Databases
Tools ➤ Database ➤ Mailing Labels*	New	Mailing Labels
Tools ➤ Database ➤ Report*	New	Report Generation
Tools ➤ Map ➤ Color/Pattern Settings	New	Mapping
Tools ➤ Map ➤ Insert Object	New	Mapping

Table I.1: New and revised commands since Release 4 *(continued)*

Command	Type of Change	Reference Topic
Tools ➤ Map ➤ Ranges & Title	New	Mapping
Tools ➤ Map ➤ Redraw	New	Mapping
Tools ➤ Map ➤ Set Redraw Preferences	New	Mapping
Transcript ➤ Make Button	New	Buttons

Compatibility with 1-2-3 for DOS Files Is now implemented in the File ➤ Open and File ➤ Save As commands. On performing either of these commands, selecting the file type from a drop-down list determines the format to be read or written. A separate translation step, such as using the Translate utility, is not required.

The data file structure of 1-2-3 Release 5 for Windows uses the extension .WK4, one which combines in a single file the Release 3 structures .WK3 (worksheet) and .FM3 (format) that were used with Release 3 for DOS and Release 1 for Windows. (See *Opening a File* and *Saving a File* in Part II.)

Multiple Currency Formats For a variety of countries can now be displayed in the same sheet. Release 5 includes 43 different predefined currency formats, as well as one that can be defined by the user. (See *Currency Formatting* and *Number Formatting* in Part II.)

One-Step Charting Can be performed by selecting the range to be charted, clicking the Draw A Chart SmartIcon, and then clicking the upper-left corner of the chart location in the sheet. A bar chart in the default size will be generated. Instead of clicking the corner of the chart, you can drag the area for a custom-sized chart. (See *Charting* in Part II.)

Previewing Multiple Pages   Is a new feature of the File ➤ Print Preview command that can also be performed by clicking the Print Preview SmartIcon. You can now move forward or backward through the stack of pages that will be generated from a multipage sheet or set of sheets. (See *Previewing Printouts* in Part II.)

Flexible Print Compression   Is an option of the File ➤ Print command, by which columns, rows, or both can be compressed or expanded so that a worksheet can be printed on a single page. Charts and other graphic objects can also be expanded or compressed. (See *Printing* in Part II.)

Collections   Are multiple, nonadjacent selections of cells or ranges. A collection can be formed by holding down the Ctrl or Shift keys as you click or drag each cell or range in the selection. Charting, editing, application of styles, printing, SmartSum, and fill-by-example operations can now be performed on collections.

Fast Range Formatting   Permitting the copying of number and appearance formatting from one range to another has been made possible by adding the Copy A Range's Styles SmartIcon to the Default SmartIcon set. (See *Fast Range Formatting* in Part II.)

SmartMasters   Available whenever you select File ➤ New are a new set of interactive templates (.WT4 files) that can be used to create typical reports. The templates are implemented as fill-in-the-blank forms, with all required formatting and formulas already done. Some SmartMasters included with Release 5 are Loan Amortization, Marketing Plan, Personal Budget, and Expense Report. You just fill in the data and print.

An empty SmartMaster called *Shell* is provided for you to create your own fill-in-the-blank templates. (See *SmartMasters* in Part II.)

Mapping   Which makes it possible to generate geographic maps from worksheet data, is a major addition to 1-2-3 capabilities. (See *Mapping* in Part II.)

@Functions That are new to Release 5 include @CELL, @CELLPOINTER, @DATESTRING, @DURATION, @IRR, @ISEMPTY, @MAXLOOKUP, @MDURATION, @MINLOOKUP, @MIRR, @NETWORKDAYS, @NEXTMONTH, @SETSTRING, @STRING, @SUMNEGATIVE, and @SUMPOSITIVE. (See *Part III: @Function Reference.*)

Easier Database Query Is made possible in Release 5 by implementing all database commands as a sequence of dialog box selections, eliminating the need for you to create specially structured tables in your sheet.

ODBC Database Access Adheres to Microsoft's Open Database Connectivity specification. This feature can be used to link a 1-2-3 sheet to an external database, as well as to issue commands to it without having the database manager installed locally. The DataLens drivers for dBASE, Paradox, SQL Server, and Lotus Notes are provided with Release 5. Also available are DataLens drivers for Informix, OS/2 DB/2, Oracle 6 and 7, and an ODBC driver for manipulating 1-2-3 worksheets from an external database manager. (See *Databases, External Databases, Querying Databases,* and *SQL* in Part II.)

SmartSuite Integration The program has built-in interfaces to the Lotus applications Improv, Ami Pro, SmartPics, and Freelance Graphics, as well as to electronic mail systems cc:Mail, Lotus Notes, and other systems that adhere to VIM or MAPI. A link is also provided to Lotus ScreenCam, a multimedia recording application that can be used to create on-screen presentations that include animation and sound.

As of Release 5, the 1-2-3 application has built-in links to Organizer, a calendar and contact manager, and Approach, a personal database manager. Several new 1-2-3 commands are available for manipulating Approach files: Tools ➤ Database ➤ Dynamic Crosstab, Tools ➤ Database ➤ Form, Tools ➤ Database ➤ Mailing Labels, and Tools ➤ Database ➤ Report. (See the following entries in Part II: *Cross-Tabulation, Forms for Databases, Mailing Labels,* and *Report Generation.*)

Dynamic Cross-Tabulation   Works much like the Tools ➤ Database ➤ Crosstab command to summarize data in tables, but provides more interaction and flexibility of table composition. This new feature requires the installation of Lotus Approach on the same system. (Notice that Release 5 has *two* commands for cross-tabulation: Tools ➤ Database ➤ Dynamic Crosstab involves an external link to Approach; Tools ➤ Database ➤ Crosstab works only within 1-2-3. See *Cross-Tabulation* in Part II.)

Pasting Worksheets into Ami Pro   Can be done by the drag-and-drop method between 1-2-3 and Ami Pro. In addition, the 1-2-3 worksheet will automatically match the appearance formatting of the Ami Pro document.

Version Manager Enhancement   Improves workgroup approaches to using multiple versions of worksheet ranges. Ranges can be mixed and matched to create scenarios. Lotus 1-2-3 tracks changes to versions by user name, date, and comments. The worksheet display can be switched among versions in the Version Manager dialog box, which appears when you select Range ➤ Version. Worksheet templates can be distributed electronically among workgroup members, and versions and scenarios from different sources can be merged. Lotus 1-2-3 can also compare the results produced by different versions and generate a report.

Versions can be distributed and shared within a Lotus Notes network by saving the worksheet file with the extension .NS4. (See *Version Manager* in Part II.)

Part II

Command and Topic Reference

This portion of the book covers most of the core capabilities of Lotus 1-2-3 for Windows. Entries are usually titled by the task you want to perform rather than by the command you would use to achieve it. If you want information on a specific command, look it up in the index, where you will find the page number of the topic that covers the command procedure.

In 1-2-3, most commands appear as items in pull-down submenus from the menu bar. Proceeding from left to right across the menu bar, the pull-down menus are: File, Edit, View, Style, Tools, Range, Window, and Help.

Also covered in this portion are pull-down commands, or *submenu items*, within the Chart, Query, and Transcript menus. These menus are context-sensitive—they appear only when you are working on tasks that use those commands. For example, the Chart menu appears when you create a chart (Tools ➤ Chart), Query when you have created a database table (Tools ➤ Database ➤ New Query), and Transcript when you have opened the macro Transcript window (Tools ➤ Macro ➤ Show Transcript).

If there is a SmartIcon equivalent for a command, it is pictured in its entry here. (Remember that there are many more SmartIcons available than appear in the Default Sheet set. See the entry *SmartIcons* and the inside front and back covers of this book.)

@FUNCTION SELECTOR

 The *@Function Selector* is a button that appears at the left side of the contents box. Clicking on the @function selector activates a drop-down menu of @function names. Select the name of an @function from the list to paste the name, syntax, and placeholders for arguments in the contents box.

To Choose and Paste an @Function

1. Select the cell that will hold the @function.

2. Click the @Function Selector button. A drop-down menu of @function names will appear.

3. Click an @function name. Its name and required syntax will be pasted into the contents box.

or

Select List All, select an @function name from the @Function List dialog box, and select OK.

4. Click the contents box to activate the insertion point.

5. Edit the text of the function formula, providing actual references for argument placeholders.

6. Click ✓, press ↵, or click outside the cell to accept the formula and insert it into the selected cell.

OPTIONS By default, the drop-down menu lists the six most commonly used @functions: SUM (addition total), AVG (arithmetic average), ROUND (rounding of decimal values), IF (conditional statement), TODAY (insert today's date), and NPV (net present value of an investment).

To edit this list, select the Menu button in the @Function List dialog box in step 3. Select a name to add from the @Functions list and select the Add button. Or, highlight an item to delete in the Current Menu list and select the Remove button. Highlight an item in the Current Menu list and select the Separator button to insert a separation line in the menu just below that item.

 **SEE ALSO**   *Entering Data, Formulas, Part III: @Function Reference*

ADDING RECORDS TO A DATABASE

The command Tools ➤ Database ➤ Append Records adds new records to the end of a database table.

To Append Records to a Database Table

1. Select a range containing records to add to the table. (See *Notes* below.)

2. From the Tools pull-down menu, select Database.

3. From the Database cascade menu, select Append Records.

4. If you wish to override the range you selected in step 1, type a reference in the Append Records From text box, or click its button and use the Range Selector pointer to drag a range in the sheet.

5. Click the upper-left cell of the database table (using the Range Selector pointer) to insert a range reference in the To Database Table text box, *or* type the reference.

or

To append records to a previously named table, press F3, select the name of the table, then select OK.

6. Select OK to close the Append Records dialog box.

NOTES Lotus 1-2-3 appends the records as additional rows at the bottom of the database table. Use Range ➤ Sort to put the records in order.

In step 1, the first row must contain the same field names (column headings) as the database table, or the error message "Invalid Field Name" will appear.

To append records, you must have previously inserted new, blank records immediately under the last record in the table. If the appended records are outside the named range of the original database table, you must use the Range ➤ Name command to reset the range definition to include the new rows. (See the entry *Naming a Range*.)

SEE ALSO *Naming a Query, Naming a Range, Sorting Database Records, Sorting a Range*

ADD-INS

The Tools ➤ Add-In command enables you to load or remove *add-ins*, or auxiliary programs and files, to or from memory. Add-ins may be provided by third-party vendors and can include application programs, as well as additional @functions or macros that extend the capabilities of 1-2-3. Add-ins are stored as files with the extension .ADW.

To Load or Remove an Add-In

1. From the Tools pull-down menu, select Add-In.

2. The Add-In dialog box appears. Select the file name of the add-in from the Add-Ins list box.

3. To bring the add-in into memory, select the Load button.

or

To remove a previously loaded add-in, select Remove.

or

To remove all add-ins currently in memory, select Remove.

4. If you selected Load, the Load dialog box will appear. Select the file name of the add-in, then OK. The add-in will be read into memory from disk.

5. To run the add-in, select its menu command *or* press its macro key.

 NOTES You might need to navigate the directory system in the Load dialog box. The default subdirectory for .ADW files is 123R5W\PROGRAMS\ADDINS.

If you remove an add-in containing @functions that are referenced in formulas in the current worksheet, the result of the formula will be displayed as *ERR*.

SEE ALSO *Part III: @Function Reference*

ADDRESSING

Addressing is the notation in formulas and other references by which cells and ranges can be located within a worksheet and worksheets located within files. The *address* of a cell is composed of the letter of its column (such as *A*), followed by the number of its row (such as *1*):

A1

A range is a rectangular block of cells defined by two cell addresses—the upper-left corner (cell address A1) and the lower-right corner (H3). The separator .. is used between the addresses to mean "and all cells through and including," as shown in the example below:

A1..H3

If a file contains multiple worksheets, the sheet is indicated by its letter or name, followed by a colon and preceding the cell address or range reference. For example, the following notations refer to a cell and a range in sheet A:

A:A1
A:A1..A:H3

 SEE ALSO *Ranges*

AGGREGATING DATABASE QUERIES

After you have selected a query table you created using the command Tools ➤ Database ➤ New Query, you can use the Query ➤ Aggregate command to perform calculations that correlate multiple fields in the table.

To Perform Aggregate Calculations

1. Select a query table. A bold border and handles should surround the table, and the Query selection should appear in the menu bar.

2. From the Query pull-down menu, select Choose Fields. The Choose Fields dialog box will appear.

3. In the Selected Fields list, click the name of any field you wish to *exclude* from the aggregate query.

4. Select Clear.

5. Repeat steps 3 and 4 for any other fields you wish to exclude.

6. Select OK to close the Choose Fields dialog box.

7. In the query table, click the column heading of the field that will be the basis for the aggregate. The entire field (or column) will be highlighted.

8. From the Query pull-down menu, select Aggregate.

9. In the Aggregate dialog box, select a Compute operation. (See *Options*, below.)

10. Select OK.

NOTES   Results will be pasted in the column you selected in step 7, overwriting the old data. The field will be renamed <Result> Of <FieldName>, where <Result> is the type of result produced by the Compute operation you selected in step 9 and <FieldName> is the name of the original field.

If you have to analyze data in database tables, aggregating fields is faster and more efficient than using Range ➤ Analyze ➤ What-If Table with database @functions.

The query table cannot contain any computed fields.

OPTIONS   The Compute options in step 9 perform the selected operation on any item that matches the corresponding item in the basis field:

Sum   Adds the entries in the basis field, grouped by the categories of the fields aggregated in the query.

Avg   Averages the entries in the basis field, grouped by the categories of the fields aggregated in the query.

Count   Counts the number of entries in the basis field, grouped by the categories of the fields aggregated in the query.

Min   Reports the minimum value in the basis field for each of the other categories.

Max   Reports the maximum value in the basis field for each of the other categories.

 **SEE ALSO**   *Choosing Fields for a Query, Querying Databases, What-If Tables*

ALIGNMENT

The Style ➤ Alignment command can override the alignment, or justification, of labels and values specified in Style ➤ Worksheet Defaults for a selected range or query table. You can align data within a single cell or in a range.

The SmartIcons associated with alignment are shown in Figure II.1.

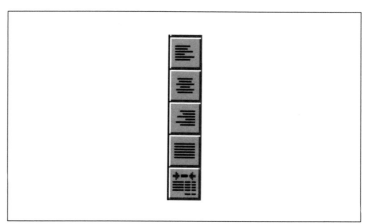

Figure II.1: SmartIcons for aligning text and data

To Align Data in a Range

1. In the current worksheet window, highlight a range for which this alignment setting will apply.

2. From the Style pull-down menu, select Alignment.

3. In the Alignment dialog box, select the label alignment for Horizontal, Vertical, and Orientation. (See *Options* below.)

4. Optionally, select the check box Across Columns to position labels relative to the entire range.

5. If you wish to redefine your selected range, type a reference in the Range box or click its button and drag a range in the sheet with the Range Selector pointer.

6. Select OK.

To Align Text in a Text Block

1. Select a text block you created with the Tools ➤ Draw command.

2. From the Style pull-down menu, select Alignment.

or

Click on the text box with the right mouse button to bring up the quick menu. Select Alignment.

3. In the Alignment dialog box, select an Align All Text option: Left, Center, Right, or Evenly Spaced.

4. Select OK.

NOTES   This command has the effect of changing the label prefix character of text data. (See *Entering Data*.)

If you are working on a file in Group mode, this command affects the same range in all sheets.

Any label that is longer than the column width is aligned left automatically.

OPTIONS   If you select Across Columns in step 4 of "To Align Data in a Range," the options refer to the left and right range boundaries. The labels should be in the far left column of the range.

 New Feature   Available with Release 5 is a new SmartIcon for this purpose: Center Across Columns.

Options in the Alignment dialog box in step 4 are covered below:

Horizontal   Select options relative to the edges of the cell that contains the label:

General   Aligns text or labels to the left and values to the right.

Left   Aligns text or labels and values to the left.

Center   Centers text or labels and values.

Right   Aligns text or labels and values to the right.

Evenly Spaced   Justifies and evenly spaces text, but ignores labels ending in punctuation marks (./:/!/?).

Across Columns   Justifies a label according to one of the options above and in relation to the full width of the range in which it is selected. For example, you can select Center and Across Columns to position a label in the horizontal center of the selected range.

Vertical   Alignment options are Top, Center, and Bottom in relation to cell boundaries.

Wrap Text   Marking this check box causes text or labels to wrap to the next line instead of being truncated at the right edge of the cell. The program adjusts the row height to fit the wrapped text.

Range   If you wish to redefine your selected range, type a reference in the Range box, or click its button and drag a range in the sheet with the Range Selector pointer.

Orientation   Allows you to set the text at any angle. Pictogram selections are the equivalents of Horizontal, Vertical, Sideways, Sideways Flipped, or Rotated Angle.

Rotation If you select Rotated Angle in the Orientation drop-down list, this option appears. It allows you to select an angle from 1–90 degrees.

 SEE ALSO *Clearing Data from Cells, Drawing, Entering Data, Styles*

ARRANGING OBJECTS

Graphic objects may be layered upon one another (*object priority*) and their positions fixed to specific locations in a sheet.

EDIT ➤ ARRANGE ➤ BRING TO FRONT,
EDIT ➤ ARRANGE ➤ SEND TO BACK

 You can arrange two or more drawn objects so that one overlays and obscures the other. Edit ➤ Arrange ➤ Bring To Front takes the selected object and places it on top of all other objects.

 Edit ➤ Arrange ➤ Send To Back places the selected object behind all other objects.

To Change Object Priority

1. Select the object by clicking on it.

2. From the Edit pull-down menu, select Arrange.

or

Select the SmartIcon from the menu bar and skip the next step.

3. From the cascade menu, select Bring To Front or Send To Back.

EDIT ➤ ARRANGE ➤ FASTEN TO CELLS

 This command anchors selected drawn objects to specific cells so that the objects will be moved, sized, or hidden if you do any of these operations on the range containing the cells.

To Fasten Objects to Cells

1. Select the drawn object(s). (See *Selecting Data and Objects*.)

2. From the Edit pull-down menu, select Arrange ➤ Fasten To Cells. The Fasten To Cells dialog box will appear.

3. Select either Attach Object To Top Left And Bottom Right Cells *or* Top Left Cell Only.

4. Select OK.

OPTIONS There are the two options in the dialog box in step 3, (each is represented by a SmartIcon):

Top Left And Bottom Right Cells Fixes the object for moving, sizing, or hiding to the corners of the range to which it is fastened.

Top Left Cell Only Fixes the object for moving only, fastening it only to the upper-left corner of the range.

SEE ALSO *Drawing, Flipping Objects, Grouping Objects, Locking Objects, Rotating Objects, Selecting Data and Objects*

ATTRIBUTES

Attributes of text and text objects include the options Normal, Bold, Italics, Underline, and Color.

⊙ **SEE ALSO** *Fonts and Attributes*

AUDITING

The command Tools ➤ Audit produces a report or highlights cells and ranges showing formulas, formula precedents, cell dependents, circular references, and links to files or OLE applications. The purpose is to track possible sources of calculation error in the sheet.

SmartIcons associated with worksheet auditing are shown in Figure II.2.

To Audit a Sheet

1. To find formula precedents or cell dependents, select the cell or range that contains the formula(s) or value(s) you want to audit.

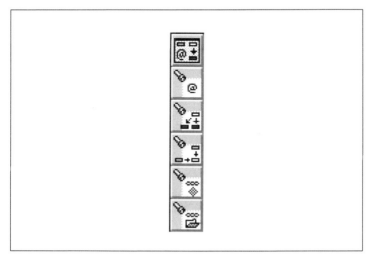

Figure II.2: SmartIcons for auditing worksheets

2. From the Tools pull-down menu, select Audit. The Audit dialog box will appear.

3. Select an Audit option for the type of worksheet reference or relationship to be checked. (See *Options* below.)

4. Select either Produce A Selection (highlighting audit items) *or* Report At A Range to be inserted in the sheet. (See *Options*, below.)

5. For the Limit Audit To option, select Current File or All Files (open or linked to the current file).

6. Select OK to start the audit.

NOTES   Your option selections in the Audit dialog box must match the type of reference being checked. For example, if you specify to limit the audit to All Files, you must also specify to produce a Report. The other option, Selection, which highlights references in the sheet, can be done only in one file at a time.

 A *circular reference* is a formula that refers to itself, either directly (by specifying its own cell address or name) or indirectly (by specifying another formula that, in turn, specifies the first one). When a formula contains a circular reference, the status bar displays the button shown here.

To locate the cell that contains the circular reference, click the Circ button, and the cell pointer will move to the cell.

If Tools ➤ Audit finds only one circular reference, the program highlights or produces a report on cells in the circular path. If Audit finds multiple circular references, the Multiple Circular References dialog box appears. If Audit finds multiple branches in a circular reference, the Multiple Branches dialog box appears.

When you use Tools ➤ Audit to generate a selection that finds multiple references, each cell identified in the audit is treated as a separate range. Press Ctrl-⏎ to move the cell pointer to the next range, Ctrl-Shift-⏎ to move to the previous range.

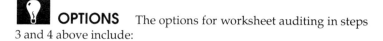 **OPTIONS** The options for worksheet auditing in steps 3 and 4 above include:

Audit Options control the types of items in the sheet to be examined:

> **All Formulas** Finds all cells that contain formulas.
>
> **Formula Precedents** Finds all cells that are referred to in a formula that you select in step 1.
>
> **Cell Dependents** Finds all cells containing formulas that refer to the cells you select in step 1.
>
> **Circular Reference** Finds all cells that refer to themselves in circular references.
>
> **File Links** Finds all cells containing formulas that refer to cells in other 1-2-3 files.
>
> **DDE Links** Finds all cells with references that link the current file to other Windows applications.

"Produce A" Options Refer to the type of results produced by the audit:

> **Selection** Instead of generating a separate report, simply highlights cells in the current file only that satisfy the Audit options.
>
> **Report At Range** Generates a report listing all cells found in the audit, one item per cell from top to bottom, left to right. Specify a blank Range to hold the report (you need only specify the starting, or upper-left, cell in the range that will hold the report). Type a reference or click the button to activate the Range Selector pointer and drag a range in the sheet.

"Limit Audit To" Options Can be selected to control the extent of the audit:

> **Current File** For Selection options. Do not specify this option if you are searching for file or DDE links.
>
> **All Files** For the Report option, provided that multiple files are open or the current file contains references to other files, whether open or closed.

 **SEE ALSO**   *Circular References*

AXES OF CHARTS

The command Chart ➤ Axis sets parameters for the X, Y, and optional second Y (2nd Y) axes of the currently selected chart. (In vertical orientation, the Y axis is on the left, the 2nd Y on the right. In horizontal orientation, the Y is on the bottom, the 2nd Y on top.)

To Define Chart Axes

1.   Select a chart by clicking on it. (Small square handles should surround the entire chart window.)

2.   From the Chart pull-down, select Axis.

3.   From the cascade menu, select X, Y, or 2nd Y.

4.   In the X/Y/2ndY Axis dialog box, set options for Axis Title, Scale Manually limits and intervals, and Show Tick Marks At. Enter an axis title in the Axis Title text box by typing it in or by referencing the contents of a cell. Indicate whether tick marks should be shown at Major or Minor Intervals, and how frequently they should appear. (See *Options*, below.)

5.   Also in the dialog box, select the Options button to indicate the Type Of Scale, the Axis Units, and the Units Title. Then select OK.

6.   When you have finished making settings in the Chart X/Y/2ndY Axis dialog box, select OK.

NOTES   Use dual Y axes when plotting two or more data ranges that are measured in different units or orders of magnitude. The objective of dual Y plotting usually is to look for corresponding fluctuations and trends. For example, company income in millions of dollars might be plotted against the Y axis, with U.S. Gross National Product in trillions of dollars against the 2nd Y.

If you use dual Y axes, use a color-coding scheme to associate each data range with its Y axis. Also for clarity of presentation, include only two data series in the chart—one for each Y axis.

If you define scale boundaries with the Scale Manually options, do not specify an upper limit that is less than the lower limit. If you do, the program will simply display a blank chart window.

If you make both X and Y axes logarithmic (log-log plotting), don't specify a linear (Standard) second Y axis. Semi-log and log plots are typically used in scientific and engineering applications to show data items of widely different magnitudes in the same data series on the same chart. However, avoid these formats if your audience is unfamiliar with logarithmic plotting.

If you enter a range name when specifying axis title and name of units (step 4), the program will use the label in the first cell in the range.

You can also assign X-axis labels by using the Chart Ranges command.

Notice that the arrow pointer changes shape over each portion of the chart. Holding down the right mouse button at these locations enables context-sensitive quick menus.

 OPTIONS   The following options can be set in the dialog box in step 4:

Axis Title   Enter a text string up to 256 characters long, or enter a cell address or range that contains a label. Selecting the Cell check box enables a selection pointer so you can to point to a range on the worksheet.

Scale Manually   The default is Automatic (no entries here), which calculates a scale to fit the data range. If you define the scale manually by marking check boxes here and entering numeric values, you must enter both Upper and Lower Limits for the data. (If you set only the Upper Limit, 1-2-3 will use the defaults for the other options.) You can also select the scale for the Major and Minor Intervals (scale divisions).

Show Tick Marks At   Enables you to show tick marks at major or minor intervals.

Place Label Every *N* Ticks   Enter a whole number *N* for the interval at which labels will be placed on the scale. The label will be the axis value at that point. For example, type 5 to display a label at every fifth tick.

Options   Selecting the Options button in step 5 lets you set the following additional Chart Axis options:

Type Of Scale   Specify Standard (linear), Logarithmic, or 100%. If you make only one of the scales (X or Y) logarithmic, a semi-log plot will be generated. Specify both as logarithmic for log-log plotting. The 100% option generates a scale from 0–100 percent and plots data values as percentages of the maximum.

Axis Units   The default is Automatic, which calculates the order of magnitude for scale values based on the data range. If you select Manual, you must enter an exponent (power of 10) in the corresponding box ($-95 <= E <= 95$). For example, on a scale 0–20,000, you would enter an exponent of 4 to indicate 10^4.

Units Title   Enter a text string as a label for scale units (for example, Millions) or enter a cell address or range that contains a label. Selecting the Cell check box enables a selection pointer so you can point to a range on the worksheet.

 SEE ALSO   *Charting, Labels for Chart Data, Legends for Charts, Naming a Range, Number Formatting, Ranges for Charting, User Setup*

BACKSOLVER

Backsolver is a special feature of 1-2-3 that calculates the value of the variable in a formula when you specify the desired result of the formula. This feature is invoked by the command Range ➤ Analyze ➤ Backsolver. The calculated value must correspond to a cell address in the selected formula.

To Use Backsolver

1. Move the pointer into the worksheet that contains the formula.

2. From the Range pull-down menu, select Analyze.

3. From the Analyze cascade menu, select Backsolver.

4. The Backsolver dialog box appears. In the Make Cell text box, enter the address of the cell that contains the formula.

5. In the Equal To Value text box, enter the result value.

6. In the By Changing Cell(s) text box, enter the address of the cell to be solved.

7. Select OK.

NOTES Backsolver substitutes values for the variable cells you specify in step 6 until the formula results in the value you specify in step 5. It then displays the solution value in that cell. For the Backsolver to work, the result of the formula must depend on that cell; there cannot be another variable in the formula. The value you enter in step 5 must be numeric or a formula with a numeric result.

You can restore the original value in the test cell (reverse the result of using Backsolver) if you select Edit ➤ Undo before executing another command.

SEE ALSO *Solver*

BUTTONS

Buttons are graphic objects that, when clicked, start *macros*, or automated command sequences. By creating a button and assigning a macro to it, you can create a menu-driven application complete with multiple buttons for user selections.

Buttons are created by the command Tools ➤ Draw ➤ Button. A macro can be assigned to a button by the command Tools ➤ Macro ➤ Assign To Button, which is initiated automatically each time a new button is drawn.

> *New Feature*   A button can be both created and assigned to selected commands in the macro Transcript window by the command Transcript ➤ Make Button.

TOOLS ➤ DRAW ➤ BUTTON

This command can be used to create a new button as a graphic object in a sheet.

To Draw a Button

1. From the Tools pull-down menu, select Draw.

2. From the Draw cascade menu, select Button.

3. With the mouse, drag the rectangular shape of the button in the sheet.

   or

   Click once at the button location to accept the default button size.

4. The Tools ➤ Macro ➤ Assign To Button command will be started automatically. Follow the program prompts to assign a macro to the new button.

TOOLS ➤ MACRO ➤ ASSIGN TO BUTTON

This command is started automatically after you complete Tools ➤ Draw ➤ Button, or you can use it to reassign a previously defined button to a different macro.

To Assign a Macro to a Button

1. To create a button, use Tools ➤ Draw ➤ Button, as described above.

2. Select the object that represents the button in the sheet.

3. From the Tools pull-down menu, select Macro.

4. From the Macro cascade menu, select Assign To Button.

5. The Assign To Button dialog box appears. In the Assign Macro From drop-down box, select an option. Assign the Range containing the macro by typing a reference, or select from existing named ranges in the list box.

or

In the Enter Macro Here box, type a sequence of macro commands.

6. In the Button Text text box, type a label that will appear on the button.

7. Select OK.

NOTES   If the button represents a macro that is contained in a range in the sheet, you can edit the macro directly as long as you do not change its range name.

If you typed the macro commands into the text box in step 5, the macro is embedded in the button and you must reopen it for editing. Select the button and reopen the macro listing by pressing Shift or Ctrl and clicking on the button. Right-click the button to display the quick menu and select Assign Macro. (After you have assigned a macro to it, clicking the button runs the macro.)

Macros can also be assigned to custom SmartIcons. (See *SmartIcons*.)

TRANSCRIPT ➤ MAKE BUTTON

 This command creates a button in the worksheet and assigns selected macro commands in the Transcript window to that button.

To Create a Button from Recorded Macro Commands

1. From the menu bar, select Tools ➤ Macro ➤ Record.

2. Execute the commands and actions of a new macro.

3. From the menu bar, select Tools ➤ Macro ➤ Show Transcript. The Transcript window will open, showing the recorded macro commands.

4. In the Transcript window, drag the set of commands you wish to assign to a button.

5. From the menu bar, select Transcript ➤ Make Button.

6. Click the location of the new button in the worksheet. A default-sized button will be created.

or

Drag the boundaries of a custom-sized button in the sheet.

7. In the dialog box that appears, edit the commands in the Enter Macro Here box, if you wish.

8. Optionally, type a label for the button in the Button Text box.

9. Select OK to close the dialog box. Clicking the button in the sheet will run the macro.

SEE ALSO *Arranging Objects, Fonts and Attributes, Locking Objects, Macros, SmartIcons*

CHARTING

Most spreadsheets can take more data than can be shown as a single chart. For best results, select one or two columns or rows as data sets that show meaningful trends, then follow these steps.

New Feature   Creating a default chart can now be done by selecting the range, clicking the Draw A Chart SmartIcon, then clicking the top-left corner of the chart area in the sheet.

To Create a Chart

1. Highlight the range in the current worksheet that contains the data to be graphed.

2. Click the Draw A Chart SmartIcon.

or

From the Tools pull-down menu, select Chart. The pointer icon will change to a small chart symbol.

3. For a default-sized chart, click the upper-left corner of the chart area in the sheet.

or

Drag a range that will contain a custom-sized chart.

4. Optionally, customize the chart by selecting commands from the Chart pull-down menu.

or

Point to a chart object with the mouse, and press the right mouse button. A quick menu will appear. Select a command for changing the options of the selected object.

NOTES   If the selected range contains more rows than columns of data, 1-2-3 plots the data by columns; otherwise, the program plots the data series by rows. When determining whether or not the number of columns exceeds the number of rows in the range selected, 1-2-3 excludes blank columns and rows.

To create a worksheet range for most types of charts, including the default vertical bar chart, make the first column the X range and put data ranges A–W in columns 2–23.

After step 3, a chart is generated automatically with default options as a vertical bar chart, including default title, axis labels, and legend. The program will use the column headings and row labels included in your data range to create the title, legend, and axis labels.

When the default chart appears, it is preselected, or surrounded by handles. The Chart selection appears in the menu bar so that you can select the commands in its pull-down menu to change chart options and appearance.

Charts in Releases 4 and 5 for Windows are embedded in .WK4 files and are not stored separately.

◉ **SEE ALSO** *Chart Types, Naming a Chart, Preferred Chart Type, Ranges for Charting*

CHART TYPES

The command Chart ➤ Type permits you to set the chart type, or plotting method, for an existing chart that you created with the Tools ➤ Chart command. Optionally, you can specify the orientation of axes and the placement of the chart, and generate a table of data values. SmartIcons are also available for quick selection of chart types (see Figure II.3).

New Features Release 5 includes three new SmartIcons for these chart types: Mixed, 100% Vertical Bar, and 100% Horizontal Bar.

To Change the Chart Type

1. Select a chart by clicking on it. (Small square handles should surround the entire chart area.)

2. From the Chart pull-down, select Type.

3. In the Chart Type dialog box, select one of the Types option buttons, as well as the Orientation of axes. (The default is Vertical unless you specifically select Horizontal.)

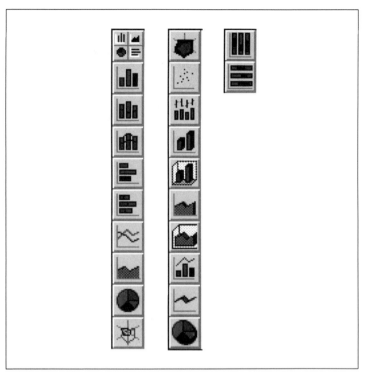

Figure II.3: SmartIcons for selecting the chart type. (To access
icons not in the default toolbar, select a chart in the
sheet and then select Tools ➤ **SmartIcons.)**

Placement of the chart is Automatic unless Manual is specifically selected. (See *Options*, below.)

4. For the selected chart type, a set of plotting styles will appear in the dialog box as graphic buttons. Select one of
them or accept the default (shown as a depressed button).

5. Optionally, to generate a table in the chart of data values
for each chart data series, mark the Include Table Of Values check box. (This option is not available for some chart
types. See *Options*, below.)

6. Select OK.

To Change the Chart Type Using SmartIcons

1. Select a chart by clicking on it. (Small square handles should surround the entire chart window.)

2. From the set of SmartIcons, select the icon for the chart type you want (see Figure II.3, above).

3. If you selected the Mixed chart type, perform steps 3–5 above for each data series to be charted.

NOTES The Default Chart set of SmartIcons will appear as a row of buttons across the top of the sheet window when you select a chart.

Each range of data items to be plotted is called a *data series* or *chart data range*. Each chart can include up to 23 data series, designated A–W. These series can be linked to worksheet data ranges by the Chart ➤ Ranges command. Exceptions are single Pie and 3D Pie charts, which have only one plotted data series (chart range A).

Use line plots to show continuous variation and trends. Use bar charts to compare performance of different entities. Use area plots to emphasize volumes with trends. Use XY (scatter) charts to plot discrete points gathered through experimental or statistical means. The default chart type is a bar chart.

Graphing conventions normally plot time on the X axis and quantity (such as dollars or units) on the Y axis. Use Vertical orientation (the default) for most types of graphs unless you are plotting *durations*, or time spans, as horizontal bars.

If a worksheet range is used to define the X axis and the labels are too long, the program automatically staggers the positions of the labels along the axis.

In stacked plotting, data ranges are layered on one another so that the Y values of each range are cumulative with respect to preceding ranges.

Selecting a chart and clicking the right mouse button once will activate a quick menu with Type as a selection.

OPTIONS   Options in the Chart Types dialog box include the following:

Types   Select one option button to determine the chart type or plotting method.

Line   Links data points with a continuous line. One line is plotted for each data series A–W. (See the information on *Plot Style* just below .)

Area   Links data points with a continuous line and shades the area beneath it with color and/or hatching. One area is plotted for each data series A–W.

Bar   Shows Y data values as separate (clustered) bars (each value in the data series as a separate bar) or layered (stacked) bar segments (stacked in a single bar). One bar or bar segment is plotted for each data series A–W.

Pie   Plots *one data range* (usually A) as slices, or *wedges*, of a circular area, or *pie*.

XY   Plots discrete points in a scatter chart. A point or symbol is plotted for each value in data series A–W.

HLCO   Shows data series A–D as *H*igh, *L*ow, *C*lose, and *O*pen values respectively on a bar chart of stock prices. Data series E is plotted as a set of bars beneath the HLCO area and is typically used to plot daily volume. Data series F is plotted as a line within the HLCO area and can be used for comparisons with other financial indicators, such as interest or monetary exchange rates.

Mixed   Plots data series A–W as any combination of clustered or stacked bars, lines, or areas.

Radar   Shows the distance of individual data points from a central point. Radar charts are often used to show data uniformity, or symmetry, or to compare individual data points with a group of points.

3D Line   Shows stacked or unstacked lines with a dimensional effect. (The lines look like ribbons.) One line is plotted for each data series A–W.

3D Area   Similar to 3D Line, but with shaded (colored and/or hatched) areas between the line plots. One area is plotted for each data series A–W.

3D Bar   Similar to Bar, but with a dimensional effect. (The bars look like blocks.) One bar or bar segment is plotted for each data series A–W.

3D Pie   Similar to Pie, but with a dimensional effect on the circular area. One data range (usually A) is plotted.

Plot Style

When you make a chart type selection, a set of *icons*, or graphic buttons, appears in the dialog box for the plotting style to be used. (The Area type has only one plotting style—stacked.)

Line and XY styles   Can be continuous with points, continuous without points, or scatter (points only).

Bar styles   Can be clustered or stacked. At each X-axis division, the Clustered option shows a cluster, or close grouping, of separate bars for each Y value in data series A–W. Stacked data series A–W are placed on top of one another as segments of a single bar at each X axis division. (The bars look like stacks of building blocks.) Stacked bars can have comparison lines connecting similar ranges with the next bar. By setting Chart Axis Y options, stacked bars can be displayed as 100%, in which all bars have the same size and segments in the stack correspond to percentages of the total bar. (See *Axes of Charts*.)

Mixed styles   Include clustered bars with lines and points, clustered bars with lines, clustered bars with areas, stacked bars with lines and points, stacked bars with lines, and stacked bars with areas.

HLCO charts   Can be whisker or candlestick. The whisker style shows a vertical line for the range from high to low, with tick marks on the line for open and close. The candlestick style superimposes a thin vertical bar on the high-low line to indicate the open-to-close range.

Radar   Can have data series plotted as lines or as areas.

3D lines and areas   Can be unstacked or stacked (cumulative among data ranges).

3D bars   Can be clustered, stacked, or clustered in three dimensions. Instead of clustering bars next to one another, bars clustered in three dimensions are layered along the third dimension (a Z axis, in effect) at each X-axis division.

Pie and 3D Pie   Allow you to plot the data as slices in counterclockwise or in clockwise order, starting at 0 degrees (3 o'clock).

Orientation   Does not apply to Radar, Pie, or 3D Pie chart types. For the other types, options are:

Vertical   The default, generates a vertical Y axis and horizontal X axis. This is the conventional plotting format for showing time (X) versus quantity (Y).

Horizontal   Resets the plot orientation to show a vertical X axis and horizontal Y axis. If dual-Y plotting is done by selecting 2nd Y for any data range, the Y scale is shown along the bottom and the 2nd Y along the top of the plotting area.

Placement   The following options for positioning the chart are:

Automatic   The default, lets the program control the composition of the chart.

Manual   This option becomes available for some types of charts if you previously repositioned the chart within the chart area by dragging it. You can then reset the options to Automatic to have the program recompose the chart.

Include Table Of Values   Generates a worksheet-style table below the chart with X values in the first row, A values in the second row, B values in the third row, and so on for all data series displayed in the chart. This option is not available for Pie, 3D Pie, Radar, HLCO, and XY graphs, or for any chart in horizontal orientation.

 **SEE ALSO**   *Axes of Charts, Charting, Ranges for Charting*

CHOOSING FIELDS FOR A QUERY

 The command Query ➤ Choose Fields lets you select and order the fields in a query table and creates computed columns with formulas.

To Change Fields in an Existing Query Table

1. Select a query table. A bold border and handles should surround the table, and the Query selection should appear in the menu bar.

2. From the Query pull-down menu, select Choose Fields.

3. In the Choose Fields dialog box, the Selected Fields list box contains all of the field names in the query table. To remove a field from the Selected Fields list box, highlight it and select the Clear button. To remove all fields, select Clear All.

4. To move a field in the query table, highlight the field in the Selected Fields list box, and then press ↑ or ↓ until the field is properly placed in the list.

5. To add a field, select the Add button. In the Add Fields dialog box, select fields from the Available Fields List Box, then select OK.

6. Select OK to close the Choose Fields dialog box.

NOTES Use this Query pull-down command only after you have created a query table. To create a new query table and move or remove fields in it, see *Querying Databases.*

In the Choose Fields dialog box in step 5, if the Add button is dimmed, all available fields are listed in the Selected Fields list box. If the Add button is active, one or more of the fields has been cleared and is available for reselection.

Once you have selected OK in the Choose Fields dialog box, processing starts and you cannot interrupt the query. If you are unsure of the fields in a long query, remember to limit the number of records returned to shorten the query. Before you do this command, do Query Set Criteria and mark the Limit Records check box. Set a small number of records, and select OK.

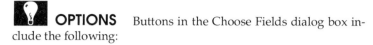 **OPTIONS** Buttons in the Choose Fields dialog box include the following:

Add Permits fields previously cleared to be added back to the list of fields to be included in the query.

Clear Removes fields from the query list.

Clear All Removes all fields from the query list, permitting you to use the Add button to reselect them individually.

Formula Permits you to Insert or Replace a computed field in the query, entering a new formula by which its entries will be calculated. The related option Show Field As permits you to name or rename an inserted or replaced computed field.

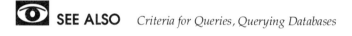 **SEE ALSO** *Criteria for Queries, Querying Databases*

CIRCULAR REFERENCES

A *circular reference* is a formula that refers to itself, either directly (by specifying its own cell address or name) or indirectly (by specifying another formula that, in turn, specifies the first one).

A circular reference is usually an error. However, certain types of repetitive, or *iterative*, calculations can be circular, provided that a limit is placed on the number of iterations. The number of iterations can be set by selecting Tools ➤ User Setup ➤ Recalculation.

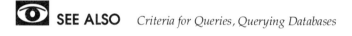 **SEE ALSO** *Auditing, User Setup*

CLEARING DATA FROM CELLS

 The command Edit ➤ Clear deletes the contents and/or removes the style of the highlighted cell or range in the current worksheet.

The command Edit ➤ Clear All applies only to macro transcripts.

EDIT ➤ CLEAR

Types of data cleared by this command include numeric values, text, graphs, formulas, and formatting. If the data is removed, the affected cells remain in the worksheet and contain blanks. New data entered into those cells will take on the current format. If the style is cleared from the cells, the data will remain. If both the data and style are cleared, new data entered into the cells will take on the default format. The SmartIcon clears *styles only* from a selected range.

To Clear a Cell or Range in a Worksheet

1. Select (highlight) the cell or range from which the contents will be cleared.

2. From the Edit pull-down menu, select Clear.

or

If you wish to remove only the data, press Del and skip step 3.

3. In the Clear dialog box, select one of the options: Cell Contents Only, Styles Only, or Both.

4. Select OK.

NOTES   In the Clear dialog box in step 3, you can enter a reference in the Range box to redefine the current selection. Or, you can click the button at the right of the box to activate the Range Selector pointer to highlight a range in the sheet.

If the selection is a chart or a drawn object, the Clear dialog box will not appear, and the chart or object will simply be deleted.

To undo a deletion, select Edit ➤ Undo before you select any other command or press Alt-Backspace or Ctrl-Z before you make another deletion.

Using Edit ➤ Clear does not affect the contents of the Clipboard or any cells that have been protected.

To clear a chart and also move it to the Clipboard, use Edit ➤ Cut instead.

Remember that charts and drawings appear to exist on a separate layer—"above" the cells of the worksheet. So, if you clear data from a range, any chart or drawing that is positioned over that range will be unaffected.

As a shortcut, select the entire chart or a data range and click the right mouse button, then select Clear from the quick menu that appears.

EDIT ➤ CLEAR ALL

Appears as a command selection in the Edit pull-down menu when the macro Transcript window is open. Select it to clear the contents of the Transcript window without affecting any macro commands you might have copied to the Windows Clipboard.

 **SEE ALSO**   *Cutting Data to the Clipboard, Undo*

CLOSING FILES

 The command File ➤ Close closes the file and document window indicated by the current position of the cell pointer.

To Close a Worksheet File

1.   Move the cell pointer to the document window that contains the file you want to close and click to make the window active.

2.   From the File pull-down menu, select Close.

3.   If the Close dialog box appears, select Yes to save the file, select No to abandon the changes, or select Cancel to keep the file open.

NOTES   You can reverse this command by performing Edit ➤ Undo before you do anything else, but remember to save your work.

The Close dialog box will appear in step 3 if you have made any changes to the file during your work session.

SEE ALSO   *Saving a File*

COLOR

Color is an attribute of text and graphic objects. Colors can also be specified for worksheet tabs, cell backgrounds and borders, and Designer Frames surrounding blocks of cells.

 **SEE ALSO** *Colors for Chart Data Plots, Lines and Object Colors, Worksheet Defaults*

COLORS FOR CHART DATA PLOTS

As an alternative to selecting chart colors by the Style ➤ Lines & Color command, Chart ➤ Numeric Color can be used to specify colors, patterns, or both according to numeric values in special ranges you set up in the sheet called the *color range* and the *patterns range*.

> *New Feature* In Release 5, the numeric color selections have been expanded from 0–15 to 0–255; numeric pattern selections from 0–15 to 0–63.

To Chart Colors by Number

1. To specify colors and patterns that automatically override the defaults, set up ranges in your worksheet that will hold color and pattern values. (See *Notes*, below.)

2. Select a chart by clicking on it. (Small square handles should surround the entire chart area.)

3. From the Chart pull-down menu, select Numeric Color.

4. In the Numeric Color dialog box, select the data series A–W for which colors or patterns will be changed.

5. Select the Range holding the color values and select the Range holding the pattern values.

6. Select OK.

NOTES   Each cell in the colors or patterns ranges should contain a different value from 0–255 for colors, 0–63 for patterns. The values you assign to each data series will determine the color and pattern used for its plot, such as bars or lines, in the chart.

Note also that a standard VGA display can show only 16 different solid colors, including black and white. Custom colors, if used, are dithered, or shown as multicolored patterns of dots. If you have a 256-color VGA display card in your computer, you will have more solid colors from which to choose.

The 64 available patterns can also be applied to graphic objects by using the Style ➤ Lines & Color command.

To set colors and patterns manually instead of by number, click the line, bar, slice, or area in the chart, then click the right mouse button and select Lines & Color.

SEE ALSO   *Lines and Object Colors*

COLUMN WIDTH

   The command Style ➤ Column Width sets the width of a specified column or columns in a worksheet. Optionally, you can reset the width to a global default value.

To Set Column Width

1.   In the current worksheet window, highlight a range containing the columns to be adjusted.

   or

   With the mouse, move the pointer to the column-letter heading, drag the right column border to the desired width, and skip steps 2–5. (The program must be in Ready mode.)

2. From the Style pull-down menu, select Column Width.

3. In the Column Width dialog box, enter the new width in characters (1–240) in the Set Width To text box. *Or* select Fit Widest Entry *or* Reset To Worksheet Default. (See *Options* below.)

4. If you wish to redefine your selected range, type a reference in the Columns box, or click its button and drag a range in the sheet with the Range Selector pointer.

5. Select OK.

NOTES   When the worksheet file is in Group mode, this command affects all sheets in the file.

The number of characters that can be displayed in a column depends on both the width setting in step 3 and the current font size. For example, you can display more characters in a given width by reducing the font size. The default is a 9-character column width in Arial or Arial MT 12 point. (See *Worksheet Defaults*.)

If the adjacent cell to the right contains data, the program truncates the display of any label that does not fit in the specified column width. Otherwise, if the adjacent cells are blank, the label is run across them.

For correct display of numeric values, the column must be one character wider than the value format. If a value as formatted will not fit in the specified width, the program displays asterisks (*******) in place of the value. To adjust the display format instead of column width, use Style ➤ Number Format.

OPTIONS   The following are Options in the column width dialog box in step 3.

Set Width To   Enter a number from 1–240 for the column width.

Fit Widest Entry   Widens the column width to fit the largest cell entry.

Reset To Worksheet Default Returns the column width to the setting made with Style ➤ Worksheet Defaults ➤ Other Column Width, which affects all columns not explicitly reset.

◉ SEE ALSO *Fonts and Attributes, Number Formatting, Row Height, Worksheet Defaults*

COPYING DATA TO THE CLIPBOARD

The command Edit ➤ Copy copies the data, formatting, or both contained in a highlighted cell or range in the current worksheet to the Clipboard, a scratch-pad memory area in Windows that can be used to pass data among different documents and programs.

To Copy Data and/or Formatting to the Clipboard

1. Highlight the cell or range from which data will be copied.

2. From the Edit pull-down, select Copy.

or

Press Ctrl-C or Ctrl-Ins.

NOTES To both delete data from the current worksheet and move it to the Clipboard in the same operation, use Edit ➤ Cut instead. Copied data is retained on the Clipboard until you perform Edit ➤ Copy again or Edit ➤ Cut, either in 1-2-3 or in another Windows program. The Clipboard can be used to move data among 1-2-3 worksheets or among applications in Windows. To retrieve data from the Clipboard into the current 1-2-3 worksheet, use Edit

➤ Paste. (In some cases, to retrieve formatting as well, you must select Edit ➤ Paste Special instead.)

Edit ➤ Copy can also be used in conjunction with the Windows features of the Clipboard and DDE/OLE to establish data links among Windows documents and applications. (See *Linking* and *Pasting Linked Data*.)

👁 **SEE ALSO**   *Cutting Data to the Clipboard, Linking, Opening a File, Pasting Data, Pasting Formats and Objects, Pasting Linked Data, Saving a File*

COPYING DATA IN A SHEET

Can be performed by the drag-and-drop method with the mouse, or in various ways by the commands Edit ➤ Copy Down, Edit ➤ Copy Right, Edit ➤ Copy Back, Edit ➤ Copy Forward, Edit ➤ Copy Up, and Edit ➤ Copy Left.

COPYING USING DRAG-AND-DROP

Copying can be done with the mouse by holding down the Ctrl key and dragging.

To Copy Data Using Drag-and-Drop

1. Select the cell or range to be copied.

2. Move the mouse pointer to the border of the selection until it changes to a small hand symbol.

3. Press the Ctrl key *and* press and hold down the left mouse button. The hand pointer will appear to close on the selection and a small plus sign will appear beside it, indicating that a copying operation is in progress.

4. While still pressing Ctrl and holding down the mouse button, move the pointer, dragging your selection to the new location.

5. Release the Ctrl key and the mouse button.

COPYING DATA WITH EDIT ➤ COPY DOWN

 This commands *fills,* or copies, the contents of the top cell or row in the selected range to the adjacent cells below.

To Copy Down

1. Drag the mouse to select a cell or row containing data and the range below it to be filled.

2. From the Edit pull-down, select Copy Down.

or

Click the right mouse button to activate a quick menu and select Copy Down.

COPYING DATA WITH EDIT ➤ COPY RIGHT

 This command enables you to copy the contents of a cell or column to the selected adjacent columns to the right.

To Copy Right

1. Drag the mouse to select a cell or column containing data and the range to the right of it to be filled.

2. From the Edit pull-down menu, select Copy Right.

or

Click the right mouse button to activate a quick menu and select Copy Right.

EDIT ➤ COPY BACK, EDIT ➤ COPY FORWARD

A pair of commands, these appear instead of the Copy Down and Copy Right selections when you press the Ctrl key and select the Edit pull-down menu. These commands copy the first worksheet selection to fill the entire selection in a 3D range or collection.

To Copy Back or Forward

1. Select a 3D (multiple-sheet) range or collection of ranges. (The top or the back sheet must contain data, and the rest of the selection should be blank.)

2. Hold down the Ctrl key as you select the Edit pull-down menu.

3. To copy the data from the top sheet, select Copy Back.

or

To copy the data from the back sheet, select Copy Forward.

EDIT ➤ COPY UP, EDIT ➤ COPY LEFT

A pair of commands, these appear instead of the Copy Down and Copy Right selections when you press the Shift key and select the Edit pull-down menu. These commands copy the bottom row (Up) or rightmost column (Left) in the selection to fill the entire selection.

To Copy Up or Left

1. Select a range or collection of ranges. (The bottom row or the right column must contain data, and the rest of the selection should be blank.)

2. Hold down the Shift key as you select the Edit pull-down menu.

3. To copy the data from the bottom row, select Copy Up.

or

To copy the data from the right column, select Copy Left.

NOTES   The first cell or row in the range is the data to be copied. The remaining range is the target. At least two cells must be included; the source and the target.

All of these commands overwrite the cells in rest of the selection, including hidden cells.

SEE ALSO   *Copying Data to the Clipboard, Cutting Data to the Clipboard*

CRITERIA FOR QUERIES

    The command Query ➤ Set Criteria uses criteria you specify to determine which records will be returned when processing a query table you created previously with Tools ➤ Database ➤ New Query.

To Set Criteria for an Existing Query Table

1.   Select a query table. A bold border and handles should surround the table, and the Query selection should appear in the menu bar.

2.   From the Query pull-down menu, select Set Criteria.

3.   Specify a filtering criterion that the records must meet. Select from the Field, Operator, and Value drop-down list boxes.

4.   To limit the number of records, select the And button. Repeat step 3.

5.   To expand the number of records, select the Or button. Repeat step 3.

6.   To remove an entry in the criteria selection box, pick a criterion to remove. Select the Clear button.

7.   To specify the maximum number of records, select the Limit Records check box. Enter a number with the numeric incrementor.

8.   To apply the new criteria to the query table without removing the Set Criteria dialog box, select the Refresh button.

9.   Select OK.

NOTES   You can use wildcard operators (? or *), @functions, and formulas as criteria in the Values drop-down list box.

The logical operator And can be used to limit the number of records. The logical operator Or expands the number of records. Multiple criteria can be specified with combinations of And/Or relationships. For example, a criteria could ask to show records where:

Department="Sales" *and* **City="New York"** *or*
Department="Sales" *and* **City="Los Angeles"**

The logical tests that you compose appear as statements in the Criteria box. With the mouse, you can copy or move statements you select in this box: click a statement so that a box surrounds it. Press Shift as you drag to move it within the Criteria box or Ctrl as you drag to copy it.

SEE ALSO   *Choosing Fields for a Query, External Databases, Joining Database Queries, Naming a Database Field, Querying Databases*

CROSS-TABULATION

The command Tools ➤ Database ➤ Crosstab creates a cross-tabulation table from a selected database range. The purpose of a cross-tabulation is to analyze data by correlating fields in a new way. For example, a cross-tabulation might seek to analyze spending habits by consumer groups, correlating unit sales by both age group and geographic region.

New Feature   If you have the new version of Lotus Approach installed in your system, you can use the command Tools ➤ Database ➤ Dynamic Crosstab, which permits you to rearrange Approach tables, create summaries, and report on the data. The resulting table is embedded as an Approach object icon in the worksheet.

To Make a Crosstab Table

1. Select the range that contains the database table, including the column headings (field names).

2. From the Tools pull-down menu, select Database.

3. From the Database cascade menu, select Crosstab. If the range you selected is a single cell or not a table, the Crosstab dialog box will appear. (If you have selected a valid table, omit the next step.)

4. In the Crosstab dialog box, if you wish to override the range you selected in step 1, type a new reference in the text box, or click its button and use the Range Selector pointer to drag a range in the sheet.

5. Select Continue. If you have selected a valid database table, the Crosstab Headings Options dialog box will appear.

6. In the Row Headings list box, select the field in the original database table that contains the row headings for the new crosstab table.

7. In the Column Headings list box, select the field containing the column headings for the new table.

8. Select Continue. The Crosstab Data Options dialog box will appear.

9. Select the Summarize Field from which values will be calculated for the crosstab table.

10. Select the Calculation method: Sum, Average, Count, Minimum, or Maximum.

11. Select Continue. The cross-tabulation will be inserted as a table in a new sheet in the current document.

NOTES   The database range you select in step 1 must contain at least three columns and two rows. Remember that, for the program to regard your selection as a valid database table, the column headings in the first row must be field names, and each row must contain one record.

The new Dynamic Crosstab feature, which uses the command Tools ➤ Database ➤ Dynamic Crosstab and a different procedure, initiates an OLE link to Lotus Approach. Approach commands are then used to manipulate the 1-2-3 table. (Press F1 in Approach for Help.) If this application has been properly installed, the following statement should appear in the [Lotus Applications] section of the file LOTUS.INI:

APPROACH=C:\APPROACH\APPROACH.EXE Lotus Approach

The device C: in this statement may be different, depending on the location of the program files.

 **SEE ALSO**   *Aggregating Database Queries, What-If Tables*

As a new feature in Release 5, multiple currency formats can be applied to the same sheet, one of which can be designated as the Default Currency format. SmartIcons for currency formatting are shown in Figure II.4.

Several of the more commonly used Currency formats can be selected by clicking the Number Format button at the left end of the status bar at the bottom of the screen.

To Apply Currency Formatting

1. Select the cell(s) to be formatted.

2. From the menu bar, select Style ➤ Number Format. The Number Format dialog box will appear.

3. From the Format listing, select Currency.

4. From the Currency listing, select one of the 43 predefined notations.

or

Select Other Country, select the Modify Symbol button, type the symbol (or its Alt code) in the Symbol box, then

Figure II.4: SmartIcons for Currency formatting.

select OK. (Optionally, select whether the symbol will appear Before or After the monetary value.)

5.   Select OK.

 NOTES   One worksheet can display any or all of the 43
available currency formats, plus one user-defined format.

In the Modify Symbol dialog box in the alternative procedure for
step 4, you can enter the ANSI/ISO code for a symbol in the current
font. Hold down the Alt key while you press the four-digit code on
the numeric keypad.

Another method is to use the Lotus Multibyte Character Set
(LMBCS) codes. Press Alt-F1 (Compose) and type the digits you
find in the LMBCS table in the user's manual.

The Default Currency style can be set by selecting Style ➤ Worksheet Defaults. When you select Currency in the Format options,
another drop-down box labeled Currency will appear, from which
you can select the default format. If you set the option here, all
numbers you enter in the current document will be displayed as
monetary amounts. (The Modify Symbol button is also available
here for entering custom symbols.)

👁 **SEE ALSO**   *Number Formatting*

CUTTING DATA TO THE CLIPBOARD

In a single operation, the command Edit ➤ Cut both deletes data
from a highlighted cell or range in the current worksheet
and also moves the data to the Clipboard. The data then
can be retrieved to the current pointer location or a new location with the Edit ➤ Paste command.

To Cut Data to the Clipboard

1.   Highlight the cell or range from which data will be copied.

2.   From the Edit pull-down menu, select Cut.

or

Press Ctrl-X or Shift-Del.

or

Click the right mouse button to activate a quick menu and select Cut.

NOTES   To delete data without involving the Clipboard, use Edit ➤ Clear instead.

Data that can be moved to the Clipboard with Edit ➤ Cut includes text labels, numeric values, formulas, formatting, charts, and inserted or embedded objects contained within the range you select in step 1.

Clipboard data is retained until you perform Edit ➤ Copy or Edit ➤ Cut again, either in 1-2-3 or in another Windows program. The Clipboard can be used to move data between 1-2-3 worksheets or between applications in Windows. To retrieve data from the Clipboard into the current 1-2-3 worksheet, use Edit ➤ Paste. (In some cases, to retrieve formatting as well, you must select Edit ➤ Paste Special instead.)

SEE ALSO   *Clearing Data from Cells, Copying Data to the Clipboard, Pasting Data, Pasting Formats and Objects, Pasting Linked Data*

DATABASES

Within 1-2-3 are special tables from which records may be extracted and placed in a separate *query table:*

Database table   Is a range that contains one column for each field of a typical database record, ordered from left to right in the order the fields appear in the database records. The top row in the table contains column-heading labels that are used as field names. Column widths correspond to field lengths, and cell formatting controls data typing.

Query table   Is a working copy of a database table in which fields and records may be reordered or recalculated.

Additionally, it is possible to connect the 1-2-3 application to an external database application that is running in the same system under Windows or that resides on a network server or remote host.

 **SEE ALSO**   *Aggregating Database Queries, Deleting Database Records, External Databases, Finding Database Records, Joining Database Queries, Naming a Database Field, Naming a Query, Querying Databases, SQL, Updating a Database Query*

DDE

In Microsoft terminology, an abbreviation for *dynamic data exchange,* which in later versions of Windows is now encompassed by *object linking and embedding,* or *OLE.* (In effect, DDE is the *L* in OLE.) Lotus 1-2-3 Release 5 for Windows supports OLE 2.0.

 **SEE ALSO**   *Linking*

DEFAULTS

Are preselected options, which can be set for the current worksheet by using the command Style ➤ Worksheet Defaults. Optionally, if Group Mode is turned on, worksheet defaults can apply to all sheets in a file.

 **SEE ALSO** *Worksheet Defaults*

DELETING CELLS

The command Edit ➤ Delete deletes the current selection (called a *section*) or entire row(s), column(s), or sheet(s) that you specify. There is one SmartIcon for each of these alternatives, as shown in Figure II.5. Unlike Edit ➤ Clear, which removes data, formats, or both, Edit ➤ Delete removes the worksheet locations as well, relettering the columns and renumbering the rows of the sheet.

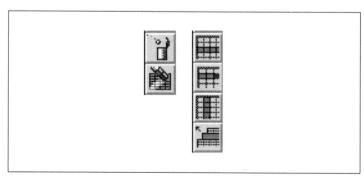

Figure II.5: SmartIcons associated with Delete

To Delete

1. Highlight the range you want to delete.

2. From the Edit pull-down menu, select Delete.

or

Press Ctrl–– (on the numeric keypad). The Delete dialog box will appear.

3. In the Delete dialog box, select Column, Row, Sheet, or Section.

4. Optionally, to override the range selection you made in step 1, use the Range Selector or enter a new range reference in the dialog box.

5. Select OK.

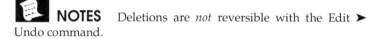 **NOTES** Deletions are *not* reversible with the Edit ➤ Undo command.

OPTIONS When using the Edit ➤ Delete command or the accelerator key Ctrl— (numeric keypad), you can make the following initial selections with the mouse:

Row To select an entire row, click the mouse on the row number on the left margin of the worksheet.

Column To select an entire column, click on the column letter on the top margin of the worksheet.

Rows And Columns You can select multiple rows and columns by dragging the mouse down the row numbers or across the column letters.

Sheet To select an entire worksheet, click on the intersection of the rows and columns at the upper-left margin of the worksheet. The intersection of rows and columns in the first sheet is labeled *A*, the second is *B*, and so on in a series.

Section To select a section, highlight a range. The Delete dialog box will appear, showing the options listed in step 3 above.

SEE ALSO *Clearing Data from Cells, Inserting Cells and Sheets*

DELETING DATABASE RECORDS

The command Tools ➤ Database ➤ Delete Records allows you to specify criteria by which records will be deleted from a database table.

To Delete Records

1. Select the range containing the database table.

2. From the Tools pull-down menu, select Database.

3. From the Database cascade menu, select Delete Records. The Delete Records dialog box will appear.

4. The range reference to the database table will appear in the Delete Records From Database Table box. If the reference is incorrect, or to select a different table, use the Range Selector *or* type a new reference here.

5. Specify a criterion for the records you want to delete. Select options from Field, Operator, and Value drop-down boxes.

6. To limit the records to delete by another criterion, select the And button. Repeat step 5.

7. To expand the number of records to delete by another criterion, select the Or button. Repeat step 5.

8. Select OK.

SEE ALSO *Adding Records to a Database, Criteria for Queries, Finding Database Records, Joining Database Queries*

DELETING RANGE NAMES

The command Range ➤ Name ➤ Delete removes the previously assigned name of a selected range address. (A *range* is a block of contiguous cells. A range address that is associated with a name is a *range name definition*.) Range names can be used instead of addresses in formulas and in any text box that requires a range entry.

To Delete a Range Name

1. From the Range pull-down menu, select Name.

2. In the Range Name dialog box, enter a name (1–15 characters) to be deleted in the Existing Named Ranges text box (or click the name of an existing range in the listing).

3. Select the Delete button to delete the name.

   or

   Select Delete All to delete all previously defined names in the current worksheet file.

4. Select OK.

NOTES When you delete a range name, the program replaces it in all formulas with the range address.

In step 2, if you type a range name to be deleted, it must be spelled the same as the existing range, but the program will ignore any differences between capital and lowercase letters.

SEE ALSO *Naming a Range, Protecting Ranges and Files, Ranges for Charting, Saving a File*

DISTRIBUTION ANALYSIS

The command Range ➤ Analyze ➤ Distribution generates a *frequency distribution* of the values in a selected range. A frequency distribution is a count of the number of data values in the range that fall within specific limits, or bounds. The range to be counted is the *value range*. The purpose is to highlight patterns in the data.

To Analyze the Distribution of a Range

1. Select two blank columns in the current worksheet. The left column is called the *bin range*.

2. Enter the limit intervals in the bin range in ascending order. Leave the right column blank—it will hold the results.

3. Highlight a *value range*.

4. From the Range pull-down menu, select Analyze.

5. From the Analyze cascade menu, select Distribution.

6. If you wish to override the value range selected in step 3, specify a range name or cell address in the Values text box.

7. In the Bin Range text box, enter the name or address of the bin range.

8. Select OK.

NOTES The program places distribution counts in the blank column to the right of the bin range. The number at the bottom of this column is a count of values greater than the bin maximum.

Enter only numeric values as bin intervals in step 2 and omit blank values and labels.

 **SEE ALSO** *Matrix Multiplication, Regression Analysis*

The command File ➤ Doc Info lets you enter descriptive data and search for document files by name, by keyword, or by contents.

To Enter Document Information

1. From the menu bar, select File ➤ Doc Info. The Doc Info dialog box will appear.

2. Type entries into any or all of the following fields, pressing Tab each time to advance to the next field: Title, Subject, Keywords, Comments, Revisions.

3. Select OK.

4. From the menu bar, select File ➤ Save or File ➤ Save As to save the worksheet file. The document information will be saved in the file as well.

5. To view the document information for the current worksheet, select File ➤ Doc Info.

NOTES The data you enter in the Doc Info dialog box can be used to search for files by using the Lotus Notes application. To enable this feature, an *application field exchange*, a special type of link between 1-2-3 and Notes, must be set up. This is a particularly convenient way of locating files within a large shared-file system or network.

If the file is a 1-2-3 SmartMaster (.WT4 extension), the title you enter here will appear in the listing each time you select File ➤ New.

Keywords, or topics for searching, must be separated by commas.

 **SEE ALSO** *Saving a File*

DRAWING

The Tools ➤ Draw <object type> commands permit you to draw graphic objects, as well as add text and macro buttons in a specified range.

SmartIcons for drawing are shown in Figure II.6.

To Draw in 1-2-3

1. From the Tools pull-down menu, select Draw.

2. From the Draw cascade menu, select the type of object you want to draw: Line, Polyline, Arrow, Rectangle, Rounded Rectangle, Arc, Ellipse, Polygon, Freehand, Text, or Button.

3. With the mouse, select the points that define the object. (See *Options*, below.)

NOTES To constrain lines to the nearest 45-degree angle, rectangles to squares, or ellipses to circles, hold down the Shift key as you draw.

When you have finished drawing an object, handles will surround it, preselecting it for further manipulation. Change object appearance and attributes with the Edit and Style pull-down commands.

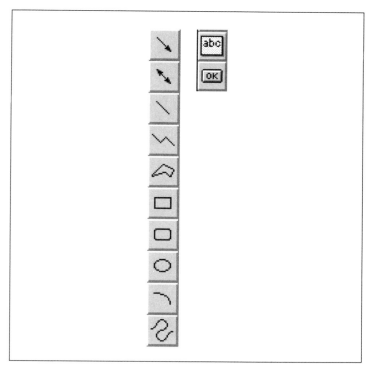

Figure II.6: SmartIcons for drawing

![OPTIONS icon] **OPTIONS**   In step 2, these are the types of graphic objects you can select and the actions used to create them:

Line   Draw a single straight line by dragging the mouse from one endpoint to the other.

Polyline   Draw a multi-sided, open shape with straight line segments, freehand line segments, or both by dragging the straight line segments and releasing the mouse button at each corner, or *vertex*, of the object. To draw freehand segments, hold down the Ctrl key as you drag.

Arrow   Draw a single straight line with an arrowhead at one or both ends by dragging the mouse from one endpoint to the other.

Rectangle Draw a rectangle by dragging the mouse to create its shape.

Rounded Rectangle Draw a rectangle with rounded corners by dragging the mouse to create its shape.

Arc Draw an arc by dragging the mouse from one of its endpoints to the other in the direction of its curvature.

Ellipse Draw an ellipse by dragging the mouse until you obtain the desired width.

Polygon Draw a multi-sided, closed shape with straight line segments, freehand line segments, or both by dragging the straight-line segments, releasing the mouse button at each corner, or vertex, of the object. To draw freehand segments, hold down the Ctrl key as you drag.

Freehand Draw a freehand object by dragging the mouse to trace its shape. (Unlike the dragging action used to create other types of objects, a freehand line is deposited along the mouse path as you drag.)

Text Draw a text block by dragging the rectangular shape of the block, then typing the text at the insertion point. Finish by clicking outside the block. (Click once instead of dragging to create a text block at the default size.) To edit text in a block, double-click on the block to reactivate the insertion point.

Button Draw a button used to run a macro by dragging the rectangular shape of the button or clicking to accept the default button size. The Assign To Button dialog box will appear. Enter the name of the macro to be associated with the button, and type a label for the button in the Button Text box. (Buttons with images typically are created as SmartIcons instead.)

⊙ SEE ALSO *Arranging Objects*, *Buttons*, *Flipping Objects*, *Grouping Objects*, *Lines and Object Colors*, *Locking Objects*, *Moving Objects*, *Rotating Objects*, *Selecting Data and Objects*, *SmartIcons*

ENTERING DATA

Entering data into cells in a worksheet can be done by typing at the keyboard.

To Enter Data

1. In the current worksheet window, use the mouse or the arrow keys to move to a blank cell that will hold the data.

2. The cell address appears in the *selection indicator* near the upper-left corner of the 1-2-3 screen.

3. Key in the data. Enter numeric values directly. Precede labels (text) with a *label prefix* if something other than default alignment (usually Left) is required.

4. The data appears in the *contents box* to the right of the selection indicator.

5. To accept the data as entered, click on the Confirm button (✓) to the left of the contents box *or* press ↵ *or* click outside the cell.

or

To cancel the new entry and restore the previous one, select the Cancel button (×) to the left of the contents box *or* press Esc.

or

To move to an adjacent cell to make another entry, press the appropriate arrow key (← → ↑ ↓). After typing that entry, press an arrow key to accept the entry and move to another adjacent cell, *or* press ↵ to accept the entry and remain in the same cell.

OPTIONS   Options for label prefixes in step 3 are the following: Align Left ('); Align Right ("); Align Center (^); Fill cell With Character (\); Omit Print Row If First Cell In Row, Otherwise Align left (¦). If text is entered without a label prefix, it will assume the default alignment of the cell, which for text is usually Left.

SEE ALSO   *@Function   Selector,   Formulas,   Keyboard Shortcuts*

EXITING 1-2-3

The command File ➤ Exit ends a 1-2-3 work session, quits the program, and returns you to Windows Program Manager.

To Exit the Program

1.   From the File pull-down menu, select Exit.

or

Double-click on the Control box in the top left corner of the 1- 2-3 window.

2.   If the Exit dialog box appears, select Yes to save the file, No to abandon the changes, or Cancel to return to 1-2-3.

SEE ALSO   *Closing Files*

EXTERNAL DATABASES

The command Tools ➤ Database ➤ Connect To External establishes a connection with a table in an external database so that you can execute subsequent Tools ➤ Database and Query commands. The command Tools ➤ Database ➤ Disconnect severs the connection.

For some database drivers, including dBASE IV, dBASE for Windows, and Lotus Notes, you must first use the Tools ➤ Database ➤ Create Table command before attempting to connect to the external database.

Having established a connection, you can select Tools ➤ Database ➤ Send Command to send a command to the external database application in its own command language and syntax.

The program feature that permits you to query external databases such as dBASE IV, Paradox, Informix, SQL Server, and IBM Database Manager is called *DataLens*. The Microsoft standard that governs connectivity among databases is called the Open Database Connectivity, or *ODBC*, specification. An auxiliary package of database drivers for 1-2-3 that adheres to the ODBC specification is Lotus Q+E.

CREATING A TABLE (REQUIRED FOR DBASE AND LOTUS NOTES)

The command Tools ➤ Database ➤ Create Table sets up a table definition that contains information on field names and widths, and data types. Optionally, you can use an existing table in 1-2-3 as a model, or you can modify the definition of an existing external table.

To Define a Table Using a Model in 1-2-3

1.   Open the 1-2-3 file that contains the database table to be used as a model. (See *Notes*, below.)

or

Build a new database table in the current worksheet.

2. Select the model table.

3. From the Tools pull-down menu, select Database.

4. From the Database cascade menu, select Create Table.

5. In the Create Table dialog box, select the database driver and then select Continue.

6. Select the database name, then select Continue.

7. When the program prompts *Enter Table Name*, type a name for the new table.

8. Select Continue.

9. The program prompts *Model Table* and displays the reference to the range you selected in step 1. If you wish to override this selection, type a reference in the text box or click its button to use the Range Selector to drag a range in the sheet.

10. In the same dialog box, if required by the database driver, type a command, or *setup string*, in the syntax of the database language for creating the new table.

11. If you wish to insert the sample records from the model table into the new database table, mark the check box Insert Records From Model Table.

12. Select OK.

NOTES In 1-2-3, a *database table* is a range that contains one column for each field of a typical database record, ordered from left to right in the order the fields appear in the database records. The top row in the table contains column-heading labels that are used as field names. Column widths correspond to field lengths, and cell formatting controls data typing.

CONNECTING AND DISCONNECTING

If the database does not exist as a table within 1-2-3, an external connection must first be established before any database operations can be performed.

To Connect to an External Database

1. From the Tools pull-down menu, select Database.

2. From the Database cascade menu, select Connect To External.

3. In the Connect To External dialog box, select the database driver name from the Select A Driver list box. Double-click the name with the mouse *or* highlight it and select the Continue Button.

or

Type the path to the database driver, database, and table (separated by spaces) in the lower text box, and skip steps 4 and 5. (For example: dBASE_IV C:\123R5W\SAMPLE\ DBASE MYTABLE.)

4. Select the database name from the Select A Database Or Directory list box. Double-click with the mouse or select the Continue button.

5. Select the table name from the Select A Table list box.

6. In the Refer To As text box, type a range name that will be assigned to the table.

7. Select OK. A linked copy of the selected database table will be pasted into the current sheet.

To Disconnect from an External Database Table

1. From the Tools pull-down menu, select Database.

2. From the Database cascade menu, select Disconnect.

3. In the Disconnect dialog box, select the table name to be disconnected.

4. Select OK.

NOTES When you select *Connect*, if prompted by the program, enter a user ID and password for the system you have selected. If the prompt appears but identification is not required, simply select OK or press ↵.

In step 3 of Connect To External, if you type a driver name that was not added to your system by Install 1-2-3, the program will prompt you to insert a diskette that holds the required driver file.

Requirements for database connection and table structure vary depending on the system being accessed.

After you disconnect from an external table, there is no further data exchange with 1-2-3, and queries and database @functions that refer to the external table may contain errors. Queries or @functions will not be updated until you reconnect to the table. To reconnect to the external table, use Tools ➤ Database ➤ Connect To External and use the same range name.

SENDING A COMMAND

Having established a connection, you can issue a command to the external database application.

To Send Commands to an External Database System

1. Connect to the external database system, as described above.

2. From the Tools pull-down menu, select Database.

3. From the Database cascade menu, select Send Command.

4. In the Send Command dialog box, select the database driver and then select Continue.

5. Select the database name, then select Continue.

6. Type the database command string in the Enter Database Command text box.

7. Select OK.

NOTES   For most database systems, the command string entered in step 6 can be any command valid in its database language. However, some DataLens drivers do not support database commands from within 1-2-3.

SEE ALSO   *Joining Database Queries, Querying Databases, SQL*

FAST RANGE FORMATTING

 As a new feature of Release 5, appearance formatting can be copied from one range to another with the Style ➤ Fast Format command.

To Apply Formatting Quickly

1.   Drag the pointer in the sheet to select the range from which formatting will be copied.

2.   From the menu bar, select Style ➤ Fast Format. The pointer will change to a paintbrush symbol.

3.   Drag the pointer in the sheet to select the range that will receive the formatting.

SEE ALSO   *Alignment, Fonts and Attributes, Lines and Object Colors, Number Formatting*

FILLING A RANGE WITH DATA

 The command Range ➤ Fill fills a range with data values generated from the starting (Start) to ending (Stop) values you enter, each value increasing according to an increment (Step).

Filling can also be done by dragging a range with the mouse (see *Filling a Range by Example*).

To Fill a Range with Incremental Data

1.   In the current worksheet, highlight a range to hold the data.

2.   From the Range pull-down menu, select Fill.

3.   The Data Fill dialog box appears. If you wish to override the range selected in step 1, specify a range name or address in the Range text box or use the range selector.

4.   Enter values for the field names Start (starting value), Increment (increment of each step), and Stop (ending value) and select an Interval.

5.   Select OK.

NOTES   This command overwrites any data in the selected range.

In step 4, valid Interval entries include numeric values, percentages, dates, or times. Start and Stop values must be of the same data type, and the Increment must be a valid way of counting that data type. Optionally, you can enter formulas, range names, or cell addresses that result in or contain values. To generate a set of values that decreases from Start to Stop, enter a negative Increment value and make sure that Start is greater than Increment. Precede the named range used as Increment with + (to increment) or – (to decrement) in the text box.

Ranges are filled top-to-bottom, left-to-right, sheet-to-sheet order.

Dates in Short International format are not valid with this command.

 SEE ALSO   *Filling a Range by Example*

FILLING A RANGE BY EXAMPLE

 Can be done with the mouse by dragging a range that contains numeric or calendar values. For example, you can drag the number 1 to generate 2, 3, 4, 5. You can drag the date value Monday to generate Tuesday, Wednesday, Thursday, Friday. Or you can specify a different increment by dragging two values, such as 1 and 3 to generate 5, 7, 9, 11.

Or, starting with data you include in a range, the command Range ➤ Fill By Example automatically fills in a sequence of characters. The example you give 1-2-3 creates a pattern for the sequence. For example, if the upper-left cell contained the label *January*, 1-2-3 would automatically fill in *February*, *March*, *April*, and so on to the end of the range.

To Fill a Range by Dragging

1.   Enter the first value in the sequence of values you want to generate.

or

To generate values by a specific increment, enter the first two values in the sequence in consecutive cells.

2. Select the cells that hold the values.

3. Move the pointer to the lower-right corner of the selection until sets of rightward- and downward-pointing triangles appear beside the pointer.

4. Press the left mouse button and keep holding it down as you move the mouse to the end of the range of cells to be filled.

5. Release the mouse button.

To Fill a Range by Example

1. In the current worksheet, enter the value or label in the first cell in the sequence. (To increment values, see *Notes* below.)

2. Highlight a range to hold the data. (Include the cell in step 1 as the starting value.)

3. From the Range pull-down menu, select Fill By Example.

 NOTES This command overwrites existing data.

To increase the values in the sequence by 1, the first cell in the range should contain an integer as a starting value.

To create a sequence that increments the data by a value other than 1, the first *two* cells in the range must contain the data to calculate. The filled data will be incremented by the difference of these two data items. If the difference is a numeric, positive value, the data will be increased by that amount; if negative, the data will be decreased.

Calendar labels, such as names of days or months, can be incremented in the same way. Custom incrementing of labels requires two examples. If the sequence in the first and second cells in the range is unclear (MONDAY and FEBRUARY, for example), 1-2-3 only uses the first cell to calculate the sequence. Without a two-cell custom sequence, 1-2-3 fills the range with the data in the first cell.

You can create a custom Fill sequence that is stored externally in the file FILLS.INI. When any list item is in the first cell in a range, 1-2-3 automatically enters all the other items in this external file, in the order they appear in your custom list.

 **SEE ALSO**   *Filling a Range with Data*

FINDING DATABASE RECORDS

The command Tools ➤ Database ➤ Find Records locates records in a database table using criteria you specify.

To Find Records

1. Highlight the range that contains the database table.

2. From the Tools pull-down menu, select Database.

3. From the Database cascade menu, select Find Records. The Find Records dialog box will appear.

4. Specify a criterion for the records you want to find. Select from Field, Operator, and Value drop-down list boxes.

5. To limit the records to find by another criterion, select the And button and repeat step 4.

6. To expand the number of records to find by another crite- rion, select the Or button and repeat step 4.

7. Select OK.

NOTES   Once a record has been retrieved, you can edit it for further processing. Press F2 (Edit) to edit the record. To move to the next matching cell in the current record, press ↵. To move to the

previous cell in the record, press Shift-↵. To move to the first matching cell in the next record, press Ctrl-↵. To move to the first matching
cell in the previous record, press Shift-Ctrl-↵. To complete editing,
press ↵ in the last matching cell in a record. To remove the highlight
from the selected record, press Esc.

 SEE ALSO *Criteria for Queries*, *Querying Databases*

FINDING AND REPLACING DATA

The command Edit ➤ Find & Replace searches for your
specified string of characters in labels, formulas, or both in
a worksheet, or searches for a string and replaces it with
another you specify.

To Search for and (Optionally) Replace Strings

1. If you wish, highlight a restricted search range.

2. From the menu bar, select Edit ➤ Find & Replace.

3. In the Find & Replace dialog box, type the string you wish
to find in the Search For text box.

4. Also in the dialog box, select one of the option buttons:
Find (to simply locate) or Replace With (to enter a replace-
ment string).

5. If you selected Replace With in step 4, type the replace-
ment string in the Replace With text box.

6. Select a option button to define the scope of the search:
Include Labels, Formulas, or Both.

7. The range you selected in step 1 should appear in the Range field of the dialog box. You can enter a new range name or address in the text box. Selecting All Worksheets instead tells 1-2-3 to search all the cells in all the work-sheets of the open file(s).

8. Select OK.

9. If found, the first occurrence of the string will be high-lighted in the worksheet. Choose one of the *Options* (see below), or select Find Next to find the next occurrence or Close to end the search.

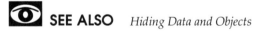 **NOTES**   Edit ➤ Find & Replace cannot be used to search for data values. Searching is limited to alphanumeric text (labels) and formulas.

This command will find strings in cells for which the format is Hid-den, but it will ignore hidden columns or worksheets that were marked with the Style Hide command.

In step 3, the search string is limited to 512 characters.

OPTIONS   If you selected Replace With in step 4, the first occurrence of the string will be highlighted in the worksheet. Select one of the option buttons: Replace (this occurrence only), Re-place All (all occurrences without asking you), Find Next (without replacing the current item), or Close (quit searching).

SEE ALSO   *Hiding Data and Objects*

FLIPPING OBJECTS

The command Edit ➤ Arrange ➤ Flip Left-Right flips the selected chart or drawn objects horizontally so they appear backward. The command Edit ➤ Arrange ➤ Flip Top-Bottom flips the selected chart or drawn objects vertically so they appear upside down.

You can manipulate each object individually, or you can start by clicking the Select All Objects SmartIcon to rearrange all objects at once.

To Flip an Object

1. Select the object(s) you wish to flip.

2. From the menu bar, select Edit ➤ Arrange.

3. From the cascade menu, select Flip Left-Right *or* Flip Top-Bottom.

 SEE ALSO *Rotating Objects, Selecting Data and Objects*

FONTS AND ATTRIBUTES

 The command Style ➤ Font & Attributes can change the font of displayed text in a selected range, as well as set attributes Bold, Italics, Underline, and Color.

To Change Font Settings

1. In the current worksheet window, highlight a range of cells to be formatted.

2. From the Style pull-down menu, select Font & Attributes.

3. In the Font & Attributes dialog box, select one of the previously installed fonts and point sizes shown in the (Type) Face list box and the Size list box.

4. If you wish to redefine your selected range, type a reference in the Range box, or click its button and drag a range in the sheet with the Range Selector pointer.

5. Optionally, select any of the attribute check boxes: Bold, Italics, or Underline.

6. If you select Underline in step 5, select a line style from the drop-down box: Single, Double, or Bold.

7. Optionally, select any Color from the drop-down color palette.

NOTES If you don't need to change the font, a fast way to set Bold, Italic, or Underline is by using the SmartIcons for these effects. Select the range and then simply click on the icon.

Face and Size settings can also be changed by clicking buttons in the live status bar at the bottom of the screen. (See *Status Bar.*)

SEE ALSO *Charting, Column Width, Gallery of Styles, Naming and Applying a Style, SmartIcons, Status Bar, Worksheet Defaults*

FOOTERS

Footers are text strings that appear at the bottom of printed pages.

SEE ALSO *Headers and Footers, Page Setup*

FORMS FOR DATABASES

 The command Tools ➤ Database ➤ Form starts the Lotus Approach application and creates a data form within it by which records in a 1-2-3 database table can be viewed and updated.

Note: This command requires installation of Lotus Approach 3.0 or higher on the same system.

To Use an Approach Form on a 1-2-3 Database

1. In 1-2-3, select the database table.

2. From the menu bar, select Tools ➤ Database ➤ Form. A message box will appear. If necessary, use the Range Selector to reselect the range that contains the database table.

3. Select OK. Approach will start, and its Form Assistant will open, permitting access to the selected 1-2-3 database table.

4. Use Approach commands to manipulate records in the database. (Click the ? button or press F1 for help on procedures in Approach.)

5. When you are finished working with the form, from the Approach menu bar, select File ➤ Exit And Return. Approach will terminate and you will be returned to 1-2-3.

or

From the Approach menu bar, select File ➤ Close And Return. The Approach application will remain open but inactive, and you will be returned to 1-2-3.

- The Approach form will be embedded in the 1-2-3 sheet as an OLE button.

6. In 1-2-3, select File ➤ Save or File ➤ Save As to save both the worksheet and the embedded Approach form in the same .WK4 file.

NOTES Double-click the embedded button in 1-2-3 to restart Approach. If the records in the database have changed since you last opened the form, the form will be updated automatically.

Approach permits only 256 characters in a database field, but 512 are permitted in 1-2-3. Approach will use only the first 256 characters of each text item.

SEE ALSO *Databases, Querying Databases*

FORMULAS

In 1-2-3, a *formula* is a set of calculations containing variables that result in a single data value. Variables can include cell and range addresses, as well as range names. Calculations contained in formulas can include arithmetic operations, logical operations, and @functions. In 1-2-3, @functions are keywords that stand for predefined formulas (see Part III).

To Enter a Formula into a Worksheet

1. Move the pointer to a blank cell that will hold the formula.

2. The cell address appears in the selection indicator near the upper-left corner of the 1-2-3 screen.

3. Key in the formula. If the formula begins with a cell address, precede it with a plus sign (+). To make the result of the formula negative, precede it instead with a minus sign (–).

4. The formula appears in the contents box to the right of the
selection indicator (see Figure II.7).

5. To accept the formula as entered, click on the Confirm button (✓) to the left of the contents box, or press ↵.

or

To enter a new formula, select the Cancel button (×) to the
left of the contents box, or press Esc.

or

To move to an adjacent cell to make another entry, press
the appropriate arrow key (← → ↑↓).

6. When you accept the formula, its result appears in the cell
in the worksheet.

NOTES   Cell addresses in formulas can be relative, absolute, or mixed (see *Ranges*). However, when a range name is used in
a formula, its range definition must include either relative *or* absolute addresses; they cannot be mixed. The program automatically
adjusts relative addresses to allow for your insertions, deletions,
moves, or copying of cells.

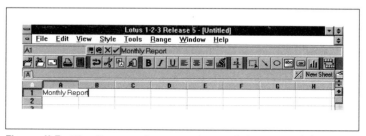

Figure II.7: The Contents box near the top-left corner of the 1-2-3
screen shows data entries as you key them in. Select
the × button to cancel or the ✓ button to confirm an
entry.

Do not include spaces within formulas. If you have entered a formula incorrectly or it refers to an invalid address, *ERR* will be displayed in its cell, or the program will sound a warning beep and the entry will not be permitted.

When calculated, formulas are evaluated in left-to-right order. Also, certain kinds of operations will precede others. Arithmetic operations are evaluated first (multiplication and division are done before addition and subtraction), then logical operations, then *string concatenation* (combinations of letters to form longer labels). As in arithmetic, the order of evaluation can be changed by enclosing items to be evaluated first in parentheses. Multiple pairs of parentheses, or nested formulas, are permissible.

A formula in one worksheet can include a reference to another file, creating a link to the external file. A file reference within a formula is a file name enclosed in double angle brackets << >>. A path preceding the file name is optional. This file reference normally would proceed a range reference (address or name) in a formula.

 OPTIONS   Formulas are of three general types:

Numeric Formulas   Numeric formulas evaluate to values. They contain arithmetic operations and @functions that evaluate to numbers, dates, or times. These are the arithmetic operators, in order of precedence:

    ^ (exponential)

    + or − (signed values)

    * (multiplication)

    / (division)

    + (addition)

    − (subtraction)

Logical Formulas   Logical formulas use the logical operators (in order of precedence: =, <, <=, >, >=, <>, #NOT#, #AND#, #OR#) in statements that result in either TRUE or FALSE. If TRUE, 1 is displayed in the cell. If the result is FALSE, 0 is displayed.

String Formulas   A string formula operates on *labels*, or text strings. (Label data contained in cells must be preceded by label prefixes. See *Entering Data*.) String formulas *concatenate*, or combine by stringing together, cell addresses that contain labels. A string formula uses the operator & to indicate concatenation. *Literal strings*, or label constants, can be inserted in string formulas by enclosing them in quotation marks (" "). For example, the string formula +A1&B1&" USA" would cause the labels in cells A1 and B1 to be concatenated with the literal string *USA*.

 SEE ALSO   *Entering Data, Ranges, Part III: @Function Reference*

FREEZING TITLES

The command View ➤ Freeze Titles locks and the command View ➤ Clear Titles unlocks the column titles along the top edge of the worksheet, row titles along the left edge of the worksheet, or both. When you are scrolling through a large worksheet, freezing the column and row titles causes them to remain in view so that you can interpret the entries easily.

To Freeze Titles

1.   Select a cell below the row you want to lock as the titles.

or

Select a cell to the right of the columns you want to lock as the titles.

or

If you want to lock both row and column titles, select a cell below the rows and to the right of the columns you want lock as the titles.

2. From the View pull-down menu, select Freeze Titles. The Freeze Titles dialog box will appear.

3. Select Rows, Columns, or Both.

4. Select OK.

To Clear Frozen Titles

• From the View pull-down menu, select Clear Titles.

NOTES   If you reduce the worksheet document window to a size that causes the pointer to disappear after you freeze titles, 1-2-3 automatically clears the frozen titles. To restore them, increase the size of the worksheet window and repeat the procedure described above.

In Ready mode, use F5 (Go To) to move the cell pointer into the title area. Specifying a cell in a row or column title then displays a second set of titles immediately below or to the right of the titles. Use this second set to edit the titles. To clear the second set of titles, press PageDown and then PageUp (for rows), or Ctrl-→ and then Ctrl-← (for columns).

If you move the cell pointer into the title area when you specify a range during a command or while entering a formula (in Point mode), 1-2-3 temporarily displays a second set of titles. When you return 1-2-3 to Ready mode, the second set disappears.

SEE ALSO   *Go To, Splitting a View*

FUNCTION KEYS

Keys labeled F1–F10 on the keyboard perform specific program operations, or functions. Function-key assignments are listed in Table II.2.

Keys F11 and F12 are not used in 1-2-3. Function keys can cause other actions when used in combination with Ctrl or Alt keys. Such key combinations in 1-2-3 that are alternatives for menu commands are called *keyboard shortcuts* or *accelerator keys*.

Table II.1: Function Keys

Key	Description
Alt-F1 (Compose)	Make custom key assignments
Alt-F2 (Step)	Toggle macro Step Mode
Alt-F3 (Run)	Display list of executable macros
Alt-F4	Exit application (File ➤ Exit)
Alt-F6 (Zoom Pane)	Enlarge/shrink current window
Ctrl-F4	Close file (File ➤ Close)
F1 (Help)	Access Help system
F2 (Edit) in Edit Mode	Edit cell entries
F2 in Ready, Point, or Value Modes	Switch mode
F3 (Name)	Select from list of names for current command or formula
F4 in Ready mode	Anchor cell pointer
F4 (Abs)in Edit, Point, or Value modes	Change reference from relative to absolute or absolute to mixed
F5 (Goto)	Move pointer to specified cell or range
F6 (Pane)	Move pointer to another pane created with Window Split
F7 (Query)	Update query table

Table II.1: Function Keys (continued)

Key	Description
F8 (Table)	Repeat last Range ➤ Analyze ➤ What-If Table command
F9 (Calc) in Ready Mode	Force worksheet recalculation and file update
F9 (Calc) in Edit or Value Modes	Convert formula to value
F10 (Menu)	Activate the menu bar

Do not confuse function keys with @functions, which are the names of predefined formulas. For more information about @functions, see *Part III*.

 SEE ALSO   *Keyboard Shortcuts*

GALLERY OF STYLES

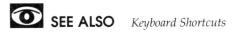 The command Style ➤ Gallery is a shortcut for formatting ranges or a collection of ranges with a predefined style that is stored as a *template* (.WT4 file).

New Feature   Release 5 includes a collection of template files called SmartMasters, which automate the creation of commonly used business forms and reports. A list of available SmartMasters will appear when you select File ➤ New (provided that you have not turned off the display of opening screens in Tools ➤ User Setup).

To Select a Gallery Template

1. Select a range or a collection of ranges. (See *Selecting Data and Objects*.)

2. From the Style pull-down menu, select Gallery.

3. From the Template list box, select the name of a style template.

4. If you wish to redefine your selected range, type a reference in the Range box, or click its button and drag a range in the sheet with the Range Selector pointer.

5. Select OK.

NOTES The Sample box allows you to preview how each style template will look before you select it.

A *collection* is two or more nonadjacent ranges. Multiple-range references can be entered in the Range text box, separated by a comma or semicolon.

SEE ALSO *Selecting Data and Objects, SmartMasters*

GO TO

The Edit ➤ Go To command lets you move quickly to a cell address, range name, chart, drawn object or query table in a an open worksheet. The ten SmartIcons associated with Go To are shown in Figure II.8.

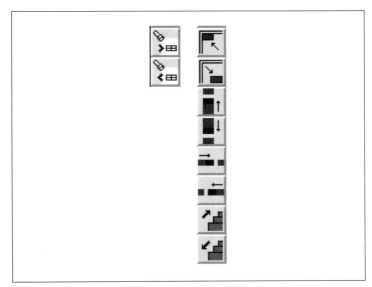

Figure II.8: The ten SmartIcons associated with Go To

To Go to a Specified Worksheet Location

1. From the Edit pull-down menu, select Go To.

or

Press F5.

2. Select the Type Of Item to display the names associated with that item: Range, Chart, Drawn Object, or Query Table.

3. Select one of the listed names or type a cell address.

4. If not in the current sheet, select the open document from the In File drop-down box where the desired item will be found.

5. Select OK.

NOTES   As an alternative, you can jump to any named cell or range in the sheet by selecting the name from the Navigator drop-down box.

The Release 4 command Range ➤ Go To has been elimi-
nated. Use the Navigator instead.

 **SEE ALSO** *Navigator*

GRIDS FOR CHARTS

The command Chart ➤ Grids sets options for display of grid lines
in chart displays and outputs. Grids can be set for the X axis, Y axis,
and the 2nd Y axis. They can be displayed only at Major Intervals,
Minor Intervals, or both.

To Set Grids

1. Select a chart by clicking on it. (Small, square handles
should surround the entire chart area.)

2. From the Chart pull-down, select Grids.

or

Click the chart border to select just the plotting area, then
click the right mouse button to activate the quick menu,
and select Grids.

3. In the Grids dialog box, select the X/Y/2ndY grid settings
for the chart from the drop-down options. (See *Notes*
below.)

4. Select OK.

NOTES Chart ➤ Grid generates lines at scale divisions
perpendicular to the axis selected: X, Y, and/or 2nd Y. The X grid
lines are vertical and the Y grid lines are horizontal. Select any combination (but usually not *both* Y and 2nd Y.)

The lines that make up the grid can be set to varying widths, colors, and styles. To change the appearance of the grids use the Style ➤ Lines & Color command. Or, click the gridlines and then click the right mouse button, then select Lines & Color from the quick menu.

 SEE ALSO *Lines and Object Colors*

GROUPING OBJECTS

The command Edit ➤ Arrange ➤ Group combines and links, or *groups*, two or more drawn objects to form a single object so that they can be manipulated and edited together. This command is a toggle that, once performed, changes to Edit ➤ Arrange ➤ Ungroup for unlinking the objects.

To Group or Ungroup Drawn Objects

1. Select the object(s). (See *Selecting Data and Objects*.)

2. From the Edit pull-down menu, select Arrange, then select Group if you selected two or more separate objects in step 1.

or

From the Edit pull-down menu, select Arrange, then select Ungroup if you selected a single, grouped object.

NOTES You can perform operations and editing on multiple objects without combining them in a group: Hold down either the Ctrl or Shift keys as you click each object to combine them in a collection before doing the operation. Remember that objects remain linked in a group, but not in a collection: when you release collected objects by clicking elsewhere in the sheet, they will not be linked to one another and must be manipulated separately.

New Feature Charting, editing, application of styles, printing, SmartSum, and fill-by-example operations can now be performed on collections.

You can perform an editing command on a collection of dissimilar objects, but the command will affect only to the objects for which it is valid.

◉ SEE ALSO *Arranging Objects, Drawing, Moving Objects, Selecting Data and Objects*

HEADERS AND FOOTERS

Specified as options of the File ➤ Page Setup command, these are text strings, appearing usually at the top and bottom of printed pages to mark dates, page numbers, file names, and so on.

To Specify Headers and Footers

1. From the File pull-down menu, select Page Setup.

2. In the Page Setup dialog box, type text in the Header and Footer fields, pressing Tab to move between the text boxes.

3. Also in the dialog box, change any of the default options settings to control the look of the page. (See *Page Setup*.)

4. Select OK.

NOTES Enter text strings to be printed as headers and footers in left, middle, and right sections at the top and bottom of each page. Leaving these fields blank clears any headers or footers that you entered previously.

OPTIONS The Insert button options are Date, Time, Page Number, File Name, or Cell Contents (specify the cell address). Click a text field, then click the button.

SEE ALSO *Page Setup, Previewing Printouts*

HEADINGS OF CHARTS

The Chart ➤ Headings command permits you to enter a title, sub-title, and footnotes to a chart.

To Add Headings to a Chart

1. Select a chart by clicking on it. (Small, square handles should surround the entire chart area.)

2. From the Chart pull-down, select Headings.

3. In the Chart Headings dialog box, enter cell references or text strings in the corresponding text boxes for Title: Line 1, Line 2; Note (footnote): Line 1, Line 2 (a title and a foot-note, one or two lines each).

or

Click the Cell check box and click a cell that holds the char-acters to be inserted as a title or footnote.

4. With the option buttons, indicate the placement of the headings: Left, Center, Right, or Manual. (See *Notes* below.)

5. Select OK.

NOTES Specifying a cell reference in step 3 will pick up the label at that address. If you specify a range rather than a single cell, 1-2-3 will use the label in the first cell of the range. Labels can be text labels, data values, or the current value of a formula at that address.

By default, titles and subtitles are centered above the chart area, and footnotes are positioned at lower-left. Chart titles and notes can be repositioned by dragging. The Manual option will be preselected in step 4 if you have dragged an existing title or note to a different position within the chart area. Use the other settings to reset a manually positioned title or notes to their default positions.

Strings of more than 250 characters can be entered, but the display of headings will be controlled by the font size specified in Chart ➤ Options ➤ Fonts. If a text line overflows the screen, it will be truncated on the right.

To change existing headings, point to the heading and double-click the left mouse button. The headings dialog box will appear. Clicking the right mouse button once will bring up a quick menu with options to Clear the headings, edit the Headings, or set Fonts & Attributes.

⊙ SEE ALSO   *Charting, Fonts and Attributes*

HELP

On-line help is available while you are working with 1-2-3. The Help item on the menu bar admits you to the same type of menu system used within Windows itself. Pressing F1 (Help) at any time displays context-sensitive help or specific information on the current task.

> *New Feature*   Descriptions of the ten most commonly performed tasks in 1-2-3 can be viewed by selecting Help ➤ Contents ➤ Top Ten Tasks.

OPTIONS   There are a variety of ways to get Help in 1-2-3. Help options appear in four places:

- As commands in the Help pull-down menu

- As commands in a menu bar just below the title bar in any open Help window

- In an *icon bar*, a row of labeled buttons, just below the menu bar of any open Help window. (The buttons are labeled Contents, Search, Back, and so on.)

- As a question-mark (?) icon in the title bar of any dialog box

The Help Pull-Down Menu   Appears in the main menu bar of the 1-2-3 program window.

About 1-2-3   Displays the version number of the program and copyright notices for 1-2-3 and for Houghton Mifflin's International CorrectSpell.

Contents   Lists commonly used Help topics. All parts of the Help system can be accessed by selecting a topic from this set of buttons. This Help window also gives information on selecting a topic. Particularly important topics include *@Functions* for detailed information on @function commands, usage, and syntax, including calculations and formulas; and *Macros* for usage, commands, and key names of 1-2-3 macros, or user-defined program routines.

For Upgraders   Lists enhancements since Release 1 for Windows. Also provides cross-references that relate 1-2-3 Release 5 selections to 1-2-3 DOS Release 3.1 (1-2-3 Classic) commands.

How Do I?   Provides information on frequently asked questions about 1-2-3, grouped by task.

Keyboard   Provides information about keyboard alternatives to commands in 1-2-3.

Search   Lets you enter a keyword for a specific topic you want to find. The program will then search through the Help index to find a match for the word you've entered. As an alternative, the Search window includes a list box of available topics. Simply click on any topic in the list box to select it.

Tutorial   Starts a set of lessons that you can work through to learn the ins and outs of spreadsheet creation. Topics include Building a Simple Spreadsheet, Working with Ranges, Enhancing a Worksheet, Creating a Chart, Printing Data, Using Multiple Worksheets, Using a Database, and Using Version Manager.

Using Help   Provides information on effectively using the 1-2-3 Help system. Information on accessing the Help system from 1-2-3, and features of the Help system are discussed.

The Help Menu Bar   Appears at the top of the document window when the text of a Help topic is displayed.

File   Opens, prints, sets up the printer, or closes Help topics or files.

Edit   Copies or pastes the text of any Help topic to the Clipboard. The Annotate command is also available for adding your own notes to the Help text.

Bookmark   Marks a Help topic so that you can return there easily for future reference.

Help   Switches to the Windows Help system. Allows the placement of Help windows always on top of 1-2-3, if you prefer.

The Help Icon Bar   Appears just below the Help menu bar when the text of a Help topic is displayed.

Contents   Provides a list of Help topics. Any part of the Help system can be accessed by selecting its topic.

Search   Lets you enter a keyword for a specific topic you want to find (see the Search entry in the section *The Help Pull-Down Menu*, above).

Back   Displays the previous topic you selected. The button is dimmed if you made no previous selections.

History   Displays a listing of topics you have consulted previously. Double-click a topic in the listing to reopen it.

Backward << and **Forward** >>   Two arrow buttons allow you to move backward or forward through the pages (windows) of the Help system. A button is dimmed if you are at that end of the list.

Help in a Dialog Box   To access Help from a dialog box, click on the question mark in the upper right-hand corner with your mouse.

 NOTES   For a one-line help message about the purpose of any SmartIcon, point to the SmartIcon and click *and hold down* the right mouse button. A description appears in a "bubble" beside the icon as long as you hold the button down.

New Feature   A bubble description will now appear if you simply pause the mouse pointer over any SmartIcon.

When you select a menu command, a one-line description will appear at the upper-left end of the program title bar.

 SEE ALSO   *Windows*

HIDING DATA AND OBJECTS

The Style ➤ Hide command hides columns and work-sheets to prevent display and printing of data.

To Hide Columns or Worksheets

1.   Select a range.

2.   From the Style pull-down menu, select Hide.

3.   In the Hide dialog box, select Column or Sheet.

4. If you wish to redefine your selected range, type a refer-ence in the Range box or click its button and drag a range in the sheet with the Range Selector pointer.

5. Choose OK.

To Redisplay after Using Style ➤ Hide

1. Select the range that includes visible cells on both sides of the hidden range.

2. From the Style pull-down menu, select Hide.

3. In the Hide dialog box, select Column or Sheet.

4. To redisplay hidden column A, type any hidden A-column cell address (A1) in the Range box.

5. Select the Show button.

6. If you are redisplaying column A, press the Home key.

To Hide Columns or Rows with the Mouse

1. At the top column border, move the mouse pointer to the right of the column letter of the rightmost column in the range that you want to hide. (Or, move to the bottom row border of the bottom range.) The mouse pointer will change to a black two-headed arrow with a black line to show the cell width.

2. Drag the two-headed arrow to the left until you are on the left column border of the leftmost column you want to hide. (Or, drag upwards to hide rows, in effect, folding the column or row back on itself.)

To Display Columns or Rows with the Mouse

1. At the top column border, move the mouse pointer to the right of the hidden column. (Or, move the top-row border of hidden rows.) The mouse pointer will change to a black two-headed arrow with a black line to show the cell width.

2. Drag to the right until the hidden column is redisplayed.
(Or, drag downwards to reveal rows.)

NOTES The range reference needs to include only one
cell in the hidden columns or worksheets to be redisplayed.

You cannot move the cell pointer to hidden columns or worksheets
in Ready mode, and you cannot enter data in them. However, formulas in hidden columns (or sheets), and formulas that refer to
data in hidden columns (or sheets) continue to work.

You may have to adjust the scroll bar to view a redisplayed column.

To unhide data in a range whose number format is Hidden, select
an alternative format in Style ➤ Number Format. To unhide data in
a worksheet whose default number format is Hidden, select an alternative format using Style ➤ Worksheet Defaults.

SEE ALSO *Number Formatting*

INSERTING CELLS AND SHEETS

The Edit ➤ Insert command inserts cells, row(s), column(s) or
sheet(s) as you specify. There are four SmartIcons associated with
Insert, as shown in Figure II.9.

 A new sheet can also be inserted by clicking this button, which is located just above the top left corner of
the document window.

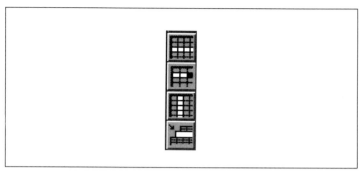

Figure II.9: The four SmartIcons associated with Insert

To Make an Insertion

1. Select a range that includes at least one cell in each of the columns or rows into which the insertion will be made.

2. From the Edit pull-down menu, select Insert.

or

Press Ctrl-+ (on the numeric keypad).

3. In the Insert dialog box, select Column, Row, or Sheet.

4. If you selected Column or Row, you can mark the Insert Selection check box to move existing data to the right (column) or down (row).

or

If you selected Sheet, choose whether the sheet will be inserted Before or After the current sheet and specify the number of sheets (Quantity) to be inserted.

5. Select OK.

 **NOTES** Any insertion causes columns to be relettered and rows to be renumbered.

⬤ SEE ALSO *Deleting Cells*

INSERTING OBJECTS

The command Edit ➤ Insert Object embeds an object created by another Windows application in the current 1-2-3 file. An
object is a set of special data types in Windows, usually
representing a collection of data in a specific format. Examples of objects are charts, drawings, bitmaps, text documents
(with or without formatting), and tables, as well as multimedia objects such as movies (animation and video) and sound recordings.

To Insert a Windows Object

1. In the current file, select a range or object to indicate the location at which the object will be inserted.

2. From the Edit pull-down menu, select Insert Object.

3. In the Insert Object dialog box, choose the object type to
be inserted.

4. Select OK. Lotus 1-2-3 will open the application associated
with the object type selected.

5. Create the object in the other application.

6. Save the object in an application file.

7. Close the application and return to 1-2-3.

NOTES Lotus 1-2-3 will place the embedded object to the
right and below the selected range or object. If the object is a document, such as a word processing file or a sound recording, it will
appear in the sheet as a button. Clicking the button starts the source
application and opens the document.

The object types you are able to select in the Insert Object dialog
box depend on the Windows applications you have installed that
support Object Linking and Embedding (OLE).

Unlike data items in external files that might simply link to locations in a sheet, a copy of the embedded object data is actually stored within the worksheet file. Therefore, the original source file need not be present after the object is inserted. However, for the object to be viewed and manipulated from within 1-2-3, the source application must be installed on the same system. Exceptions are graphic objects, which can be manipulated with the drawing tools of 1-2-3.

 **SEE ALSO** *Linking*

INVERTING A MATRIX

The command Range ➤ Analyze ➤ Invert Matrix generates the mathematical inverse of values in a square matrix. The matrix must be a square range (same number of columns and rows). For example, the inverse of N/M would be M/N.

To Invert a Matrix

1. In the current worksheet, highlight the range that holds the matrix.

2. From the Range pull-down menu, select Analyze.

3. From the Analyze cascade menu, select Invert Matrix.

4. The Invert Matrix dialog box appears. If you wish to override the highlighted selection in step 1, specify a range in the From text box.

5. In the To text box, enter a range to hold the inverted matrix. (The address of the first cell is sufficient.)

6. Select OK.

NOTES Repeating this command overwrites the range in step 5.

The matrix range must be square for use with this command. Square matrices have the same number of columns as rows. The limit is 80 columns and 80 rows. Avoid including values of greatly different magnitudes.

You can invert a 3D range. Matrices are inverted sheet by sheet; results are placed in the To range in the same worksheet.

The matrix you specify in step 4 need not be a file that is currently open. Precede the range name with a valid device, path, and file name enclosed in double angle brackets << >>.

A primary purpose of using matrix arithmetic is to solve simultaneous algebraic equations. In matrix analysis, inversion often is used as the first step in performing matrix multiplication.

 SEE ALSO *Matrix Multiplication*

JOINING DATABASE QUERIES

The command Query ➤ Join allows you to join a query to perform operations on a combination of two or more database tables.

To Join Two Tables

1. Select a query table. A bold border and handles should surround the table, and the Query selection should appear in the menu bar.

2. From the Query pull-down menu, select Join. (See *Notes* below.)

3. In the Join dialog box, select the first database table in the Join Database Table drop-down list box (or simply accept the name of the table you selected in step 1, which is preselected).

4. Also in the Join dialog box, select the second database table in the With Database Table drop-down list box (which shows the names of other query tables in the sheet).

    or

    Type the range reference of the second database table in the With Database Table box.

5. From the list below the Join Database Table box, select a field from the first table that you want to use to join the tables.

6. From the operator drop-down box between the field listings, select a logical operator: equal to (=), less than (<), greater than (>), less than or equal to (<=), greater than or equal to (>=), or not equal to (<>).

7. Select the field from the list of names in the second table that corresponds to the field in the first database table.

8. To test for multiple or alternate conditions, select the And or Or buttons and repeat steps 5–7 for another logical operation to be included in the join.

9. Select OK. The Choose Fields dialog box appears for you to select any fields you wish to exclude from the query. (See *Choosing Fields for a Query*.)

NOTES   The main purpose of the Query ➤ Join command is not necessarily to combine two tables but to perform logical operations on their fields.

The two database tables must contain a common field or data type, which are linked by the operator in the logical condition test you compose in steps 5–8. However, provided that the data types are the same, the field names can be different in the two tables. The tables must be named ranges and must be specified as such.

In steps 3 and 4, to specify an external table to which you are not yet connected, highlight the appropriate Table drop-down box and select External. Complete the connection, then select the name you assigned to the external table from the Table drop-down list.

Selecting the And or Or buttons in step 8 permits you to specify compound logical tests, which can join other query tables. The logical operator And can be used to limit the number of records. The logical operator Or expands the number of records. Multiple criteria can be specified with combinations of And/Or relationships. To include other tables, reselect the With Database Table after you select And or Or. The join criteria, or logical tests, that you have already specified appear as a series of statements in the Join Criteria box. Specifying additional criteria and/or tables allows you to *filter* a join to be more specific about conditions required for results.

 SEE ALSO   *Choosing Fields for a Query, Databases, External Database Querying a Database*

KEYBOARD SHORTCUTS

Special key combinations called *keyboard shortcuts*, or *accelerator keys*, can be used to execute 1-2-3 commands in a single operation from the keyboard, bypassing the menu system. For example, pressing Ctrl-C executes the command Edit ➤ Copy. These accelerator keys are listed in Table II.2. Accelerator-key equivalents also appear opposite the command items in pull-down menus as a letter combined with the Ctrl key.

In addition to accelerator keys, many 1-2-3 commands can be executed by making a selection from a 1-2-3 quick menu or selecting a SmartIcon.

 SEE ALSO   *Function Keys, Quick Menus, SmartIcons*

Table II.2: Accelerator and Other Keyboard Shortcuts

Key	1-2-3 Command Equivalent
Alt-Backspace *or* Ctrl-Z	Edit ➤ Undo
Alt-F4	File ➤ Exit
Ctrl— (on numeric keypad)	Edit ➤ Delete ➤ Row/Column/Sheet
Ctrl-+ (on numeric keypad)	Edit ➤ Insert ➤ Row/Column/Sheet
Ctrl-*letter**	Tools ➤ Macro ➤ Run (* Do not assign macros to any Ctrl-key combinations shown in this table)
Ctrl-B	Toggle ➤ Bold
Ctrl-C *or* Ctrl-Ins	Edit ➤ Copy
Ctrl-E	Align ➤ Center
Ctrl-I	Toggle ➤ Italic
Ctrl-L	Align ➤ Left
Ctrl-N	Reset to Normal text
Ctrl-O	File ➤ Open
Ctrl-P	File ➤ Print
Ctrl-R	Align ➤ Right
Ctrl-S	File ➤ Save
Ctrl-U	Toggle on or off single Underline
Ctrl-V *or* Shift-Ins	Edit ➤ Paste
Ctrl-X *or* Shift-Del	Edit ➤ Cut
Del	Edit ➤ Clear
F5	Edit ➤ Go To

Other Keys

↑↓	Move cell pointer up or down
←→	Move cell pointer left or right
Alt	Access menu bar commands
Alt--	Display Control menu of current window

Table II.2: Accelerator and Other Keyboard Shortcuts (continued)

Other Keys	
Ctrl-← or Shift-Tab	Move cell pointer to far left of screen
Ctrl-→ or Tab	Move cell pointer to far right of screen
Ctrl-Break	Cancel current command; Esc
Ctrl-End Ctrl-PgDn	Move to cell last highlighted in previous active file
Ctrl-End Ctrl-PgUp	Move to cell last highlighted in next active file
Ctrl-End End	Move to cell last highlighted in last active file
Ctrl-End Home	Move to cell last highlighted in first active file
Ctrl-Esc	Switch to another Windows application
Ctrl-F4	Close current window or dialog box
Ctrl-F6	Next (Graph, Worksheet, or Transcript)
Ctrl-Home	Move to A:A1
Ctrl-PgDn	Move to previous sheet in file
Ctrl-PgUp	Move to next sheet in file
End	Move to last match in Data Query Find
End ↑,↓,←, or →	Move to next cell containing data
End Ctrl-Home	Move to last nonblank cell in last sheet
End Ctrl-PgDn	Move to previous sheet, same location, nonblank cell
End Ctrl-PgUp	Move to next sheet, same location, nonblank cell
End Home	Move to bottom right of sheet

Table II.2: Accelerator and Other Keyboard Shortcuts (continued)

Other Keys	
Esc	Cancel current command
Enter, ↵	Accept entry; OK
Home	Move to cell A1
PgUp	Move up one screen
PgDn	Move down one screen
Shift-Tab	Ctrl-← or previous field in dialog box
Tab	Ctrl-→ or next field in dialog box

LABELS FOR CHART DATA

The command Chart ➤ Data Labels permits you to specify value labels for plots on charts (data points, pie slices, or bars) and to select the positions of those labels in relation to the points. Labels are taken from cells in the worksheet. Ranges that contain labels can be specified for chart data series A–W either selectively or as a group. (In a pie chart, the first data range X contains labels and the second range A is the one and only data series.)

To Specify Data Labels—Pie Charts Only

1. Select a chart by clicking on it. (Small square handles should surround the entire chart area.)

2. From the Chart pull-down, select Data Labels.

    or

    Click the right mouse button on an existing data label to activate a quick menu, and select Data Labels.

3. In the Chart Data Labels dialog box, select Show or Explode Slices. (See *Options* below.)

4. Select OK.

 **OPTIONS**   Select check boxes in step 3 to set the following options:

Show   Selecting the Values check box allows the actual values in the data range to appear in the chart. Selecting Percentages displays each value in the A range as a percentage of the total. Contents Of X Data Range shows the text label for each pie slice. Hide/Show % Using C Range shows percentages of individual slices according to values in a third (C) range: 0 to hide, blank to show.

Explode Slices   No Explosion keeps all the slices together. This is the default. All By X % allows you to specify the amount of separation among exploded slices. Using a B Range colors and/or explodes slices by values you entered previously in an optional data series B in the sheet. Values in the B range can be numeral 1–14 for colors, adding 100 to the values for exploded slices. The Manual option allows you to explode the pie by dragging slices. (Manual appears dimmed until you drag a slice with the mouse to reposition it in the chart area.)

To Specify Data Labels for all Other Chart Types

1. Select a chart by clicking on it. (Small square handles should surround the entire chart area.)

2. From the Chart pull-down menu, select Data Labels.

or

Click the right mouse button on an existing data label to activate a quick menu and select Data Labels.

3. In the Chart Data Labels dialog box, enter cell addresses or the Range Of Labels in the text box for chart data series A–W.

or

To specify labels for all chart ranges at once, select [All Ranges] from the list box.

4. From the Placement drop-down box, select the position relative to the data point or bar at which the label will be displayed: Center (the default), Right, Below, Left, or Above.

5. Select OK.

NOTES   Any Range Of Labels you specify in step 3 should contain the same number of cells as there are data values in the chart data series. That is, there should be one label for each data value.

If you choose Center, Left, or Right for label position on a bar chart, the labels are actually placed above the bars. In a stacked chart, labels are placed inside the bar segments, regardless of the position selected.

To edit a Data Label, point to the label you wish to change and double-click the left mouse button (or, click the right mouse button and select Data Labels from the quick menu). The Data Label dialog box will appear, allowing you to change that series.

OPTIONS   Settings in the dialog boxes in steps 3 and 4 include the following:

Series   Select [All Ranges] to automatically set the label range for each corresponding data series A–W in the worksheet. This option can be used in conjunction with the Chart ➤ Ranges command, by which individual ranges can be assigned to data series. Alternately, you can type range references for each data series.

Range Of Labels   Enter the addresses or names of ranges that contain labels for data series A–W. Labels can be text labels, data values, or the current results of a formula at that address. Optionally, click the button at the right end of this box to enable a special selection pointer, and click the first cell in the sheet in a range that holds the labels. The sheet layout for specifying labels by row is shown in Figure II.10. Labels can also be specified by column. As a rule, if data series are by row, so must be the labels.

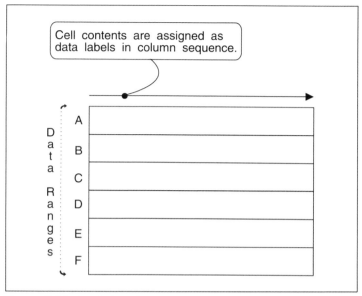

Figure II.10: Worksheet layout for Chart ➤ Data Labels ➤ Range
Of Labels, by row. For most chart types, except pies,
you can specify data ranges A–W.

Label Position   Sets the position of labels relative to data
points in line graphs, and to bars or areas, as follows: Center
(the default), Right, Below, Left, or Above.

SEE ALSO   *Clearing Data from Cells, Colors for Chart Data
Plots, Legends for Charts, Ranges for Charting*

LEGENDS FOR CHARTS

The command Chart ➤ Legend generates a legend with labeled
color/symbol/hatch codes for each chart data range. Legend text

can be entered selectively for chart data series A–W or as a group by specifying a worksheet range that contains labels.

To Create a Chart Legend

1. Select a chart by clicking on it. (Small square handles should surround the entire chart area.)

2. From the Chart pull-down menu, select Legend.

3. In the Chart Legend dialog box, select [All Ranges] to specify labels for all of the chart ranges.

or

In the Legend box, enter a range address that holds the labels.

or

Click the Cell check box and click the first cell in a range that holds the labels.

4. Specify the placement of the Legend: Right Of Plot, Below Plot, or Manual (drag the legend where you want it).

5. Select OK.

NOTES Specifying a range reference in step 3 will pick up the labels at that address. (The Cell option is not available for pie charts, for which labels must always be in the first data series X.) Labels can be text labels, data values, or the current value of a formula at that address.

By default, the legend will be displayed to the right of the chart area.

If you select [All Ranges] in a series in step 3, legend labels will be picked up from the range you specify. The contents of each cell are used as labels for the legend. Cells in the range are assigned in order to chart data series A–W.

Pie slices are labeled in order around the pie, starting with the first slice (which is at 0 degrees, or 3 o'clock). Style options with the

Chart ➤ Type command determine whether the slices are ordered counterclockwise (the default) or clockwise.

To quickly access the Legend dialog box, point to the existing legend and double-click the left mouse button. Or, click the right mouse button once to bring up a quick menu.

 **SEE ALSO**   *Axes of Charts, Chart Types, Headings of Charts*

LINES AND OBJECT COLORS

The command Style ➤ Lines & Color sets the style, color, and pattern options for text, background, borders, and frames of cells, ranges, collections, and query tables. Optionally, you can display negative values in red. This command applies to monitors and output devices that support color and overrides settings in Style ➤ Worksheet Defaults.

The three SmartIcons associated with lines and color are shown in Figure II.11.

To Specify Lines and Colors

1. In the current worksheet window, highlight a range.

2. From the Style pull-down menu, select Lines & Color.

3. The Lines & Color dialog box appears. Select any of the drop-down box options for Interior, Border, and Designer Frame. (See *Options* below.)

4. If you wish to redefine your selected range, type a reference in the Range box, or click its button and drag a range in the sheet with the Range Selector pointer.

5. Select OK.

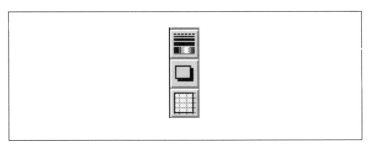

Figure II.11: SmartIcons for lines and colors

![notes icon] **NOTES** When an object is created with one of the Tools ➤ Chart or Tools ➤ Draw commands, handles appear around it so that it can be manipulated. Use Style ➤ Lines & Color at this point to recolor the object or change other style attributes.

A Sample box helps you see whether the text colors specified in step 3 contrast well with the background and pattern colors. Remember that color-blind people might not be able to read red text on a green background.

![options icon] **OPTIONS** The following options are available in the Lines & Color dialog box in step 3. On monochrome displays, colors will be shown as different shades. On 16-color displays, many of the color selections will be shown in *dithered* mode, as multicolored patterns of dots.

Interior

Background Color Can be any one of 256 colors, including white, black, 14 shades of gray, and transparent.

Pattern Select a pattern from a table of 64 patterns.

Pattern Color Overlaid on the background color, can be any one of 256 colors, including white, black, 14 shades of gray, and transparent.

Text Color Can be any one of 256 colors, including white, black, 14 shades of gray, and transparent.

Negative Values In Red Is a check box that causes negative numbers to be displayed in red.

Border

Outline Places a line along the outer edges of a range. No interior cell edges are affected.

Left Places a line at the left edge of a cell or range.

Right Places a line at the right edge of a cell or range.

All Places lines between cells, as well as around all the edges of a range.

Top Places a line along the top edge of a cell or range.

Bottom Places a line along the bottom edge of a cell or range.

Line Style Select from eight styles, including three solid, three dotted, and two dashed-and-dotted lines.

Line Color Select from a drop-down box of 16 colors.

Designer Frame   Select from a pop-up box of 16 styles.

Frame Color   Can be any one of 256 colors, including white, black, 14 shades of gray, and transparent.

Range   If you wish to redefine your selected range, type a reference in the Range box or click its button and drag a range in the sheet with the Range Selector pointer.

 SEE ALSO   *Colors for Chart Data Plots, Selecting Data and Objects, Worksheet Defaults*

LINKING

The command Edit ➤ Links establishes and maintains data links between the current worksheet and external files of other Windows applications. Links are managed under the Object Linking and Embedding (OLE) feature of Windows. Changing the data at a linked location in one file will cause the data in the other to be updated. You can specify the type of data to be transferred, as well as whether the updating will be performed automatically or manually.

To find links to open documents, click this SmartIcon.

 To find links to 1-2-3 files, whether open or closed, click here.

To Create a Data Link

1. Start the application containing the information to be linked. Open the source file and select the desired data.

2. Copy the source data to the Clipboard by using Edit ➤ Copy.

3. Open the 1-2-3 worksheet file that will hold the linked data.

4. Highlight the cell or range that will serve as the *destination range*.

5. From the Edit pull-down menu, select Links.

or

From the Edit pull-down menu, select Paste Link and skip the rest of these steps.

6. In the Links dialog box, select Create.

7. The Create Link dialog box appears. If you wish to change the default link name assigned by the program, enter new information in the Link Name text box.

8. In the Application text box, enter the name of the application program that will generate the source data.

or

From the list box, select one of the Windows applications currently open.

9. In the Topic Name text box, enter the file name (including its extension) that holds the source data.

or

From the list box, select one of the files currently open.

10. In the Item Name text box, enter the item, such as a field name, that holds the source data.

11. In the Format Name list box, select the data type or file format of the data to be transferred.

12. Select Automatic or Manual from the Update Mode option buttons.

13. If you wish to override the range selected in step 4, specify a range name or address in the Range text box.

14. Select OK.

15. To return to the worksheet, select Cancel.

To Edit an Existing Data Link

1. From the Edit pull-down menu, select Links.

2. The Links dialog box appears, with all previously established link names in the Links list box. Select the name of the link to be edited.

3. Buttons in the dialog box now are undimmed, and current settings for the selected link appear in the Information box. Select the Edit button.

4. The Edit Link dialog box appears. Reset any of the options shown by performing steps 8–13 above.

5. Select OK.

6. To return to the worksheet, select Close.

To Maintain a Link

1. From the Edit pull-down menu, select Links.

2. The Links dialog box appears, with all previously established link names in the Links list box. Select the name of the link to be maintained.

3.   Buttons in the dialog box now are undimmed, and current settings for the selected link appear in the Format information boxes. Select Update for a manual link to make data copies current in all files.

or

Select Deactivate to sever the link temporarily, until a link update is performed.

or

Select Delete to remove the link name you selected in step 2 and all its settings.

4.   To return to the worksheet, select Close.

NOTES   In most cases, data links need not be created explicitly with Edit ➤ Links. Links are also created when you use an external file reference in a worksheet formula and when you use Edit ➤ Paste Link (the alternative command step 5 of *To Create a Link*).

The OLE feature of Windows 3.1 includes some aspects of Dynamic Data Exchange, or DDE, of Windows 3.0. In Windows DDE, the application that generates a source file is called a *server* and the destination program is called a *client*. Equivalent OLE terminology is *source* and *destination*. (In effect, DDE is the *L* in OLE.)

In linking, the destination contains a pointer to the item in the source file, and any change to the item in the source will affect the copy and the destination. In embedding, a separately editable copy of the data is inserted in the destination file.

Not all applications support data exchange in both directions. Check the program documentation to be sure. Lotus 1-2-3 for Windows supports both, so a worksheet file can be both a destination (receive data from an external source) and a source (send data to an external file). When you create a link with Edit ➤ Links ➤ Create, the current worksheet is the destination file and the external file is the source.

Since dynamic data links operate between named files, both the source and the destination documents must have been saved previously to disk. (That is, you can't link to a file named UNTITLED.)

For data to be exchanged dynamically, all linked files must be open. When files are linked with a formula, the file referenced in the formula can be closed and 1-2-3 will still perform the update.

Editing data links manually usually will not be necessary. Simply redo the linking procedure. However, it may be necessary to edit the link reference if you move the source file to another directory.

Windows applications that support OLE 2.0, such as 1-2-3 Release 5, permit drag-and-drop copying and moving of data and objects between the document windows of open applications. (See "Drag-and-drop copying and moving" under *Basic Features of 1-2-3* in the Introduction, and *Pasting Worksheets into Ami Pro* in Part I.)

OPTIONS The following options appear in the Links dialog box:

Create Settings are made in the Create Link dialog box in step 7 of *To Create a Data Link*. They include:

Link Name Can be any text string. The program assigns the defaults LINK1, LINK2, and so on.

Application Is the name of any currently installed Windows application program that supports DDE or OLE.

Topic Is the file name (including extension) that holds the source data.

Item Refers to the record item or field in the source file. An item in an external worksheet might be a range address or name. In an external database field, the item might be a field name or search key. For files that have no such descriptors, enter a text string to serve as a label. If you try to leave this text box blank, an error message will appear when you select OK.

Format Refers to the data type or file format of the data to be transferred. Depending on the application, options may include Text (character data, the default), .WK3 and .WK1 (worksheet formats), Picture (Computer Graphics Metafile format), DIB (database format), or Bitmap (pixel array), as well as other types of Windows objects.

Update Mode Must be either Automatic (an update in one file triggers the corresponding update in the other) or Manual (an update occurs only when you perform Edit ➤ Links ➤ Update).

Range The location in the worksheet where the data contained in the link will be placed.

Edit Brings up the Edit Link dialog box. You can change any of the settings listed under Create above, except the link name.

Update Triggers the update of the linked data item in the destination file, using the value currently in the source file.

Deactivate Severs the selected link until a link update is executed but retains the link name and settings in the list.

Delete Removes the selected link from the list of link names, along with its format settings.

 SEE ALSO *Copying Data to the Clipboard, Inserting Objects, Pasting Formats and Objects, Pasting Linked Data*

LOCKING OBJECTS

 The command Edit ➤ Arrange ➤ Lock protects and Edit ➤ Arrange ➤ Unlock unprotects a drawn object from inadvertent changes. (If the object is locked, you can only unlock it. If the object is unlocked, your only choice is to lock it.) A single SmartIcon toggles Lock and Unlock.

To Lock an Object

1. Select the object you want to lock.

2. From the Edit pull-down, select Arrange.

3. From the cascade menu, select Lock.

To Unlock a Previously Locked Object

1. Select the object you want to unlock.

2. From the Edit pull-down menu, select Arrange.

3. From the cascade menu, select Unlock.

 **SEE ALSO**   *Protecting Ranges and Files*

MACROS

Macros are sequences of Lotus 1-2-3 command statements that are contained in worksheet cells. Macros can be assigned to SmartIcons and to special drawn objects called *macro buttons* in worksheets.

The program will generate macro commands as you perform application tasks on the command Tools ➤ Macro ➤ Record. The command Tools ➤ Macro ➤ Run plays back the macro.

To inspect the statements in a macro you have just recorded, select Tools ➤ Macro ➤ Show Transcript. The Transcript window will open, displaying the recorded commands in a separate Transcript document window. Debugging can be done with the commands Tools ➤ Macro ➤ Single Step and Tools ➤ Macro ➤ Trace.

 New Feature   A selection of commands in the Transcript window can be assigned to a new button by the command Transcript ➤ Make Button or by clicking this SmartIcon.

Custom dialog boxes for use with macros can be created and edited with the Lotus Dialog Box Editor application, which is provided with 1-2-3.

RECORDING A MACRO

 The command Tools ➤ Macro ➤ Record starts and Tools ➤ Macro ➤ Stop Recording suspends recording of keystrokes or mouse actions for macros, or predefined command sequences. The Transcript window, which can be used to inspect the recorded macro statements, is not opened; to view the results of macro recording, select Tools ➤ Macro ➤ Show Transcript.

Before you can record a macro, you must clear the contents of the Transcript window if it is open and already contains commands.

To Clear the Transcript Window

1. From the Tools pull-down menu, select Macro.

2. From the Macro cascade menu, select Show Transcript.

3. Click the title bar of the Transcript window to make it active.

4. From the Edit pull-down menu, select Clear All.

To Record a Macro

1. Clear the Transcript window, if open, as described above.

2. From the Tools pull-down menu, select Macro.

3. From the Macro Cascade menu, select Record.

4. Enter the keystrokes or the mouse actions to compose the macro.

To Stop Recording

1. From the Tools pull-down menu, select Macro.

2. From the Macro cascade menu, select Stop Recording.

NOTES During recording the mode indicator displays this notice in the live status bar:

Macro commands accumulate in the Transcript window. Each command appears on a separate line. When the Transcript window is full, the first commands are lost. To save macro commands, you must copy them from the Transcript window into the worksheet, a macro button, or a custom SmartIcon.

RUNNING A MACRO

The command Tools ➤ Macro ➤ Run permits you to select a macro and begin its execution.

To Run a Macro

1. Move the cell pointer to the first cell in a range that contains the macro to be run.

2. From the Tools pull-down menu, select Macro.

3. From the Macro cascade menu, select Run.

4. The Macro Run dialog box appears. The names of all macros in the current worksheet appear in the list box. If you wish to override the range selected in step 1, specify a macro name or address in the Macro Name text box.

5. Select OK.

OPTIONS A single-letter macro name (called a *backslash macro*) can be entered as \\N, where N is the letter. To run such a macro, simply press Ctrl and the letter key at the same time. (Do not assign key combinations that are reserved as accelerator keys, such as Ctrl-C. See *Keyboard Shortcuts*.)

OPENING AND CLOSING THE TRANSCRIPT WINDOW

 The command Tools ➤ Macro ➤ Show Transcript opens and Tools ➤ Macro ➤ Hide Transcript hides the Transcript document window.

To Show the Transcript Window

1. From the Tools pull-down menu, select Macro.

2. From the Macro cascade menu, select Show Transcript.

3. The Transcript window will open, containing all keystrokes and mouse actions you entered after you selected Tools ➤ Macro ➤ Record.

To Edit and Save a Macro

1. Start macro recording by doing Tools ➤ Macro ➤ Record.

2. Perform the commands and actions of the macro.

3. Open the Transcript window with Tools ➤ Macro ➤ Show Transcript.

4. To edit the macro, click on the window to activate it *or* press Ctrl-F6.

5. If necessary, use commands from the Edit pull-down menu to edit the macro commands in the Transcript window.

6. In the Transcript window, drag to highlight all commands in the macro.

7. From the menu bar, select Transcript ➤ Make Button and click the button location in the sheet. (Skip the rest of these steps.)

or

Select Edit ➤ Copy or Edit ➤ Cut to move the macro from the Transcript window to the Clipboard.

8. Move the pointer to the worksheet window or press Ctrl-F6 to activate it.

9. Move the pointer to the first cell of a range that will hold the new macro.

10. Select Edit ➤ Paste to copy the macro from the Clipboard into the selected location in the worksheet.

11. Select Range ➤ Name and name the new macro. (Make sure the reference in the Range box is to the whole range.)

12. If necessary, use Tools ➤ Macro ➤ Trace or Tools ➤ Macro ➤ Single Step to find errors in the macro.

13. Edit the macro to correct any errors you find.

14. Select File ➤ Save As to save the sheet that contains the macro.

To Hide the Transcript Window

1. From the Tools pull-down menu, select Macro.

2. From the Macro cascade menu, select Hide Transcript.

 NOTES If you make the Transcript window active, the Transcript selection of pull-down commands appears on the menu bar. When the Transcript window is hidden or its title bar is dimmed, the Transcript selection is removed from the menu bar.

STEPPING THROUGH A MACRO

The command Tools ➤ Macro ➤ Single Step permits you to inspect the progress of a macro while it is running. The purpose is to trace the macro's execution one step at a time to debug macro errors and to see results.

To Step through a Macro

1. From the Tools pull-down menu, select Macro.

2. From the Macro cascade menu, select Single Step.

3. Start the macro with the Tools ➤ Macro ➤ Run command, or by clicking its button or custom SmartIcon, or by pressing its backslash key (Ctrl-<letter>). (See *Notes* below.)

To Turn Step Mode Off

• Repeat the command Tools ➤ Macro ➤ Single Step. The check mark next to the Single Step menu item will be removed, and if the macro has not terminated, normal execution will resume.

NOTES   A single-letter macro name (called a *backslash macro*) can be entered as *N*, where *N* is the letter. To run such a macro, simply press Ctrl and the letter key at the same time. (Do not assign key combinations that are reserved as accelerator keys, such as Ctrl-C. See *Keyboard Shortcuts*.)

OPTIONS   When Step mode is turned on, the macro executes one step or keystroke at a time. Press any key during execution to advance to the next step. If you also turn on Trace mode with the command Tools ➤ Macro ➤ Trace, the Macro Trace window appears showing the address and contents of the current macro command. When Step mode is on, a cursor in the command string highlights each keystroke or command in the Macro Trace window as it is executed.

You can also press Alt-F2 (Step) or click the equivalent SmartIcon to start or end Step mode.

TRACING MACRO EXECUTION

The command Tools ➤ Macro ➤ Trace activates and shows the Macro Trace window, which displays the worksheet location and syntax of the macro commands being executed. The purpose is to help you find sources of error in debugging a macro.

To Activate or Close Macro Trace

1. From the Tools pull-down menu, select Macro.

2. From the Macro cascade menu, select Trace.

3. Start the macro with the Tools ➤ Macro ➤ Run command, or by clicking its button or custom SmartIcon, or by pressing its backslash key.

NOTES This is a toggle command. Selecting it the first time turns Trace mode on. Selecting it again turns Trace off. When the command is on, a check mark appears next to the Trace item in the menu.

NOTES ON EDITING MACROS

Macro commands must have the following general syntax:

{MacroName} with no arguments

or

{MacroName Argument1,Argument2,...,ArgumentN}

The macro command string, including its name and arguments, must be entirely enclosed by a set of braces {}. Optional arguments are shown in the program documentation in brackets []. (Do not use brackets in command syntax.) The following general rules apply:

- Range references can be addresses or names.

- Values, except where noted, can be numeric values, labels, formulas that generate values or labels, or range references that contain values.

- Precede a text formula with a plus sign (+).

- Literal strings must be enclosed in quotation marks " ".

- Most arguments that require string values can also be formulas that generate labels or range references that contain labels.

• With some commands, "Format" is an optional string value specifying a Clipboard format for data typing and appearing in the formula syntax as keywords: BITMAP, METAFILE, PICT, or TEXT. The value can be a literal string of the required keyword, enclosed in quotation marks, or a formula or range reference that results in a string.

Macro Command Syntax

To see the required syntax for a macro command, do the following:

1. In 1-2-3, select Help ➤ Contents ➤ Macros ➤ Macro Command Categories.

2. Select a macro command category. An alphabetical listing of commands in that category will appear.

3. Click on the name of a macro command.

4. A complete description of the command, its syntax, and application notes will appear.

5. Choose File ➤ Exit from the menu bar of the Help window.

Macro Key Names

Macro key names are used to represent keystrokes in macro recording and in macro command syntax.

The following keys are *not supported* and cannot be included in macros: Alt-Backspace (Undo), Alt-F1 (Compose), Alt-F2 (Step), Alt-F3 (Run), Caps Lock, Num Lock, Print Screen, Scroll Lock, and Shift.

Macro Key Name	Key Equivalent
{down} or {d}	↓
{up} or {u}	↑
{left} or {l}	←
{right} or {r}	→

~ between macro commands	↵
{~}	~
/ or < or {menu}	/ or <
{{}	{
{}}	}
{clearentry} or {ce}	Esc in Classic mode edit line
{zoom}	Alt-F6 (Zoom)
{backspace} or {bs}	Backspace
{file}	Ctrl-End
{prevfile} or {pf} or {file}{ps}	Ctrl-End Ctrl-PageDown
{nextfile} or {nf} or {file}{ns}	Ctrl-End Ctrl-PageUp
{lastfile} or {lf} or {file}{end}	Ctrl-End End
{firstfile} or {ff} or {file}{home}	Ctrl-End Home
{firstcell} or {fc}	Ctrl-Home
{backtab} or {bigleft}	Ctrl-←
{next sheet} or {ns}	Ctrl-PageDown
{prevsheet} or {ps}	Ctrl-PageUp
{bigright} or {tab}	Ctrl-→
{delete} or {del}	Del
{end}	End
{lastcell} or {lc}	End Ctrl-Home
{escape} or {esc}	Esc
{help}	F1 (Help)
{edit}	F2 (Edit) in Edit mode
{name}	F3 (Name)
{anchor}	F4 in Ready mode

{abs}	F4 (Abs) in Edit, Point, or Value modes
{goto}	F5 (Go To)
{window}	F6 (Pane)
{query}	F7 (Query)
{table}	F8 (Table)
{calc}	F9 (Calc) in Calc mode
{home}	Home
{insert} *or* {ins}	Ins
{pgdn}	PageDown
{pgup}	PageUp
{tab}	Tab
{select-bigleft}	Shift-Ctrl-←
{select-bigright}	Shift-Ctrl-→
{select-down}	Shift-↓
{select-firstcell}	Shift-Ctrl-Home
{select-home}	Shift-Home
{select-lastcell}	End Shift-Ctrl-Home
{select-left}	Shift-Left
{select-nextsheet}	Shift-Ctrl-PageUp
{select-pgup}	Shift-PageUp
{select-pgdn}	Shift-PageDown
{select-prevsheet}	Shift-Ctrl-PageDown
{select-right}	Shift-→
{select-up}	Shift-↑

 **SEE ALSO**   *Buttons, Keyboard Shortcuts, SmartIcons*

MAIL

The command File ➤ Send Mail sends files or selected ranges to other users of a network. All Lotus applications for Windows are "mail enabled" from the menu bar. For example, you can send a cc:Mail for Windows or Lotus Notes mail message without leaving 1-2-3.

Note: If a mail system is not installed, the program will display "Mail Not Available" if you try this command.

To Send Mail

1. From the File pull-down menu, select Send Mail.

2. Select OK to send a mail message.

3. A dialog box from your mail application appears, allowing you to type an e-mail message.

4. Select OK to close the dialog box and send the mail; you are returned to 1-2-3.

To Attach a File to a Mail Message

1. Make the file you want to send the current file by opening or activating its document window.

2. From the File pull-down menu, select Send Mail.

3. For unmodified files, mark the Attach check box.

or

For modified or unsaved files, mark the Save And Attach check box.

4. Select OK.

5. A dialog box from the mail application appears. Type a transmittal message.

6. Select OK to close the dialog box and send the mail; you are returned to 1-2-3.

To Insert a Range in a Mail Message

1. Highlight the range, drawn object, or chart to be included in the mail message.

2. From the File pull-down menu, select Send Mail.

3. Select OK.

4. A dialog box from the mail application appears. Type your message.

5. Select OK to close the dialog box and send the mail; you are returned to 1-2-3.

NOTES If you have not saved the file previously, a Save File As dialog box appears, allowing you to name and save the file.

For Lotus Notes or cc:Mail users, the Send Mail command automatically opens your mail application, if it is not open already.

An envelope icon appears in the status bar at the bottom of the screen to alert you that new mail has arrived. Click on the envelope to launch the mail program and retrieve your mail.

MAILING LABELS

The command Tools ➤ Database ➤ Mailing Labels uses the label-generation feature of Approach to create labels from a database in 1-2-3.

Note: This command requires installation of Lotus Approach 3.0 or higher on the same system.

To Generate Mailing Labels from a Database

1. In 1-2-3, select the database table.

2. From the menu bar, select Tools ➤ Database ➤ Mailing Labels. A message box will appear.

3. Select OK. Approach will start and its Mailing Label Assistant will open.

4. Use Approach commands to create the mailing labels. (Click the ? button or press F1 for help on procedures in Approach.)

5. When you are finished working with the labels, from the Approach menu bar, select File ➤ Exit And Return. Approach will terminate and you will be returned to 1-2-3.

or

From the Approach menu bar, select File ➤ Close And Return. The Approach application will remain open but inactive, and you will be returned to 1-2-3. The mailing labels will be embedded as an Approach object in the to 1-2-3 sheet as a button.

6. In 1-2-3, select File ➤ Save or File ➤ Save As to save both the worksheet and the embedded labels in the same .WK4 file.

NOTES Double-click the embedded button in 1-2-3 to restart Approach. If the records in the database have changed since you last worked with the labels, they will be updated automatically.

Approach permits only 256 characters in a database field, but 512 are permitted in 1-2-3. Approach will use only the first 256 characters of each text item.

 **SEE ALSO** *Databases, Querying Databases*

Various commands in the Tools ➤ Map cascade menu permit you to generate geographic maps from worksheet data.

INSERTING A MAP

 The command Tools ➤ Map ➤ New Map creates a new map from selected data in the sheet. (Other SmartIcons for mapping are shown on the inside back cover.)

To Generate a Map

1. Select a range in the sheet that contains one data value for each region of the map.

2. From the menu bar, select Tools ➤ Map ➤ New Map. The Map Type dialog box will appear.

3. From the list in the dialog box, select a map type.

4. Select OK.

5. If the program cannot identify one or more of the region labels in the selected range, the Region Check dialog box will appear. Select a region Name, Code, or Custom Names, and then click OK for each region, as prompted by the program. (See *Options* below.)

6. The pointer will change to a small crosshairs with a globe symbol. Drag an area in the sheet to hold the map.

or

Click the top-left corner of the map area to generate a map of default size.

The map will be generated and inserted in that area in the sheet, surrounded by handles.

7.   Optionally, drag the map in the sheet to reposition it.

8.   Click outside the map or press Esc to release the map and resume your work in the sheet.

NOTES   For best results, a worksheet range for mapping should have two columns. The first column should contain labels for the name, code, or custom name of each region in the map for which there is a data value. The second column should hold the values. Values will appear in the map as data labels in a legend that is color-coded to the regions on the map.

If the region labels are standard Names or Codes, the Region Check dialog box will not appear.

OPTIONS   As identified by labels in the sheet, regions for a given map can be any one of the following types (which can be selected as Region List Type in step 5):

Names   Standard names of states, countries, or geographic regions. For example: Missouri for a state name.

Codes   Standard abbreviations for regions. For example: MO (for Missouri).

Custom Names   Can be inserted in the Region Check dialog box by selecting the Add As Custom Name For option button and then selecting a Known Map Region from the list with which that name will be associated. For example: Show-Me-State for Missouri.

If the label is not meant to be a Custom Name, the program will insert the standard Name or Code in the worksheet cell if you select the Replace In Cell With option button, select a Known Map Region, then select OK.

CUSTOMIZING COLORS AND PATTERNS OF MAP REGIONS

The commands Tools ➤ Map ➤ Colors & Legends and Tools ➤ Map ➤ Pattern & Legends can be used to control the color or patterns assigned to map regions based on their values.

To Customize Map Colors, Patterns, or Both

Regions can have color, a pattern, or both. Controls and options in the Color Settings and Pattern Settings dialog boxes are similar.

1. Click the map area to select it. *Handles*, or small squares, will surround the map.

2. From the menu bar, select Tools ➤ Map ➤ Colors & Legend *or* ➤ Patterns Legend. The Color Settings or the Pattern Settings dialog box will appear.

3. In the Colors or Patterns drop-down box, select Manual. Then, specify a color or pattern for each region (Bin number) in the map by making selections from the drop-down palettes.

or

Select From Range in the Colors Or Patterns drop-down box and use the Range Selector to specify a range in the sheet that holds numeric color values (0–255) or pattern values (1–6).

4. Optionally, specify Values and Legend Labels by selecting Manual and typing them in the Bin boxes or by selecting From Range and using the Range Selector to specify a range that contains the values or labels.

5. Select OK.

OPTIONS Selections in the Colors & Legend and Patterns & Legend dialog boxes include these options:

Value Is If the setting in the Values drop-down box is Manual or From Range, option buttons determine whether the values entered in the Bin boxes are Upper Limit (specifying a value below which regions will have the same color/pattern, above which regions will have separate color/pattern codes) or Exact Match (shown in the map legend as they appear here, possibly overriding range values). If the Values setting is From Range, the values in the specified Range are used.

Map Viewer   Selecting this button places the selected map in its own document window, which has a menu bar with commands for manipulating the map. Among these, the command Map ➤ Add Overlay, permits you to add other maps from external files (.TV extension) as separate drawing layers.

ASSOCIATING RANGES WITH MAP FEATURES

The command Tools ➤ Map ➤ Ranges & Title can be used to select ranges in the sheet that will be associated with different features in the map.

To Control Map Features by Values in Ranges

1.   Click the map area to select it. Handles, or small squares, will surround the map.

2.   From the menu bar, select Tools ➤ Map ➤ Ranges & Title. The Ranges & Title dialog box will appear.

3.   From the Assign Range For list, select the map feature to be associated with the range: Map Regions (data values), Colors (numeric values for color selection 0–255), Patterns (numeric values for pattern selection (1–6), and Coordinates (values in the sheet for longitude and latitude at which "pin" symbols will be shown).

4.   Use the Range Selector or type a range reference in the Range box.

5.   Repeat steps 3 and 4 for each feature for which there are values in the sheet.

6.   Optionally, mark the Cell check box to pick up the label in a specific worksheet cell as a title for the map. (When you mark the check box, a Range Selector button will appear.)

or

Accept the default label shown (the current Map Type).

7.   Select OK.

SETTING REDRAW PREFERENCES

The map redrawing process can be controlled by using the command Tools ➤ Map ➤ Set Redraw Preference. The purpose of turning off automatic redrawing is to improve program performance by triggering redrawing only when the command Tools ➤ Map ➤ Redraw is selected.

To Turn Off Automatic Redrawing

1. From the menu bar, select Tools ➤ Map ➤ Set Redraw Preference. The Redraw Preferences dialog box will appear.

2. To turn off automatic redrawing, mark the Manual check box.

3. Select OK.

4. Resume your work in the worksheet. At any time, to regenerate all currently open maps, select Tools ➤ Map ➤ Redraw.

◉ SEE ALSO *Drawing, Selecting Data and Objects*

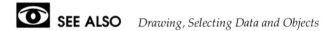

MATRIX MULTIPLICATION

The command Range ➤ Analyze ➤ Multiply Matrix multiplies one *matrix*, or array of numbers, by a second, placing the results in a third, new matrix. The first two matrices must be the same size, but need not be square.

To Multiply One Matrix by Another

1. From the Range pull-down menu, select Analyze.

2. From the Analyze cascade menu, select Multiply Matrix.

3. The Multiply Matrix dialog box appears. In the First Matrix text box, select a range for the first matrix.

4. In the Second Matrix text box, select a range for the second matrix (the multiplier).

5. In the Resulting Matrix text box, select the range for the results. (The address of the first cell is sufficient.)

6. Select OK.

 **NOTES** This command overwrites any existing data in the range in step 5.

Matrices need not be square to be multiplied, but the number of columns in the first matrix must equal the number of rows in the second matrix, and the product of these cannot exceed 6,553 cells. Neither matrix can have more than 80 cells on a side (columns or rows). The output range will have the same number of rows as the first and the same number of columns as the second.

The matrices you specify in steps 3–5 need not be in files that are currently open. Precede the range name with a valid device, path, and file name enclosed in double angle brackets << >>.

SEE ALSO *Inverting a Matrix*

MOVING OBJECTS

With the mouse, use the drag-and-drop method to move objects such as cells and range contents, charts and some chart elements, drawn objects, and query tables.

To Move an Object with Drag-and-Drop

1.   Select the object. If it is a cell or a range, a bold outline will surround it. Other types of objects will be surrounded by *handles*, or small squares.

2.   If the object is a cell or a range, move the pointer to the edge of the selection until the pointer shape changes to a small hand symbol, then hold down the mouse button and drag in the next step.

3.   Drag the object to another location in the sheet. An outline of the object will move with the pointer, and the full object will appear at the new location when you release the mouse button.

NOTES   This feature will not operate on cells and ranges unless the Drag-and-Drop Cells option is marked in Tools ➤ User Setup ➤ Options. (Marked is the default setting.)

Holding down the Ctrl key as you drag and drop causes the object to be copied rather than moved.

SEE ALSO   *Selecting Data and Objects, User Setup*

NAMING AND APPLYING A STYLE

The command Style ➤ Named Style permits you to assign names to style formatting you have established for a worksheet cell, range, or a collection of ranges. This formatting can then be applied to other selected cells by repeating the command and selecting a named style.

To Create Named Styles

1. In the current worksheet window, highlight a cell to be formatted.

2. Format the cell by making selections from the Style pull-down menu.

3. From the Style pull-down menu, select Named Style. The Named Style dialog box will appear.

4. In the Existing Styles text box, select one of the 16 Undefined Styles to define.

or

Select the name of one of your previously created Existing Styles to redefine, and select Clear to delete the existing style definition.

5. If you wish to redefine your selected range, type a reference in the Range box, or click its button and drag a range in the sheet with the Range Selector pointer.

6. Select Define.

7. Type a new description (1–19 characters) in the Style Name text box.

8. Select Close.

To Apply a Named Style

1. In the current worksheet window, highlight a range to be formatted according to the predefined style.

2. From the Style pull-down menu, select Named Style. The Named Style dialog box will appear.

3. In the Existing Styles text box, select a style name.

4. If you wish to redefine your selected range, type a reference in the Range box or click its button and drag a range in the sheet with the Range Selector pointer.

5. Select OK.

To Remove a Named Style

1. From the Style pull-down menu, select Named Style.

2. In the Named Style dialog box, select a style name.

3. Select Clear.

4. Select Close.

NOTES Named styles are stored with the worksheet file in which you created them, not as system data files. To use a named style with another file, use File ➤ Open to load both files into 1-2-3 and use the named style to format a range in the new worksheet.

A shortcut allows you to apply number formats and named styles: click the Number Format button (usually labeled Automatic) on the left end of the live status bar to display a pop-up list of existing formats.

| Automatic | | Fancy frame | Arial MT | | 12 |

Also on the status bar is the Style Selector button (third from the left), which permits you to select named styles.

When you select a number format or a named style from the status-bar pop-up menus, the selected range will be formatted accordingly.

SEE ALSO *Alignment, Column Width, Fonts and Attributes, Lines and Object Colors, Number Formatting, Row Height*

NAMING A CHART

Each time a chart is created in a worksheet, 1-2-3 assigns a name to it, such as CHART1. Use the Chart ➤ Name command to assign a more descriptive name to your chart or to rename any chart.

To Name a Chart

1.   Select a chart by clicking on it. (Small square handles should surround the entire chart area.)

2.   From the Chart pull-down menu, select Name.

3.   Enter the new name in the Chart Name text box.

4.   Select OK.

 NOTES   The first chart name will default to CHART1. Subsequent charts will be numbered accordingly in sequence. As with named ranges, you can go directly to a chart by using the Edit ➤ Go To (F5) command or the Navigator along with the chart name.

👁 **SEE ALSO**   *Go To, Navigator*

NAMING A DATABASE FIELD

   The command Query ➤ Show Field As permits you to rename a field in a database table.

To Rename a Database Field

1.   Select a query table. A bold border and handles should surround the table, and the Query selection should appear in the menu bar.

2.   Select a field in the query table by clicking the column heading.

3. From the Query pull-down menu, select Show Field As.
The Show Field As dialog box will appear showing the
field name.

4. In the Show As text box, type a new field name.

5. Select OK.

NOTES Changing a field name in a query table, or using
an *alias* name, does not change the field name in the original database table. Alias field names are useful in creating computed columns and keeping track of multiple versions. Conventions for
naming ranges apply.

SEE ALSO *Choosing Fields for a Query, Criteria for Queries, Formulas, Naming a Range, Querying Databases*

NAMING A QUERY

The command Query ➤ Name permits you to assign a new name
to a query table that you created previously with Tools ➤ Database
➤ New Query.

To Name a Query

1. Select a query table. A bold border and handles should
surround the table, and the Query selection should appear
in the menu bar.

2. From the Query pull-down menu, select Name.

3. The Name dialog box appears. In the Query Name text box,
the name of the current query table appears. In the Query
Name text box, type a new name for the query table.

4. Select the Rename button.

NOTES The conventions for naming ranges also apply here—names can be up to 15 characters long and must be unique.

Naming a query permits you to use two shortcuts:

- Passing the name as an argument to the {query-refresh} macro command runs the query and updates the query table.

- Pressing F5 (Go To) permits you to jump to a named query table.

SEE ALSO *Go To, Macros, Naming a Range, Updating a Database Query*

NAMING A RANGE

The command Range ➤ Name permits you to create or delete the name of a selected range address. (A *range* is a block of contiguous cells. A range address that is associated with a name is a *range name definition*.) Range names can be used instead of addresses in formulas and in any text box that requires a range entry. You can move the pointer location to a named range by using the Navigator.

To Create a Range Name

1. In the current worksheet window, highlight a range of cells to be named.

2. From the Range pull-down menu, select Name.

3. In the Range Name dialog box, enter a name (1–15 characters) in the Name text box.

or

Select one of the options For Cells: To The Left, To The
Right, Above, or Below to extract range names from
adjacent cells.

or

To include the selected range in the definition of an existing range name, select a name from the list box, and enter
the new range definition in step 4.

4. If you wish to override the range selected in step 1, specify a range name or address in the Range text box. (If you
select an existing name from the list box, its address
appears here.)

5. Select the Add button.

6. Create more range names by repeating steps 3–5.

7. Select OK.

To Delete a Range Name

1. From the Range pull-down menu, select Name.

2. In the Range Name dialog box, enter a name (1–15 characters) to be deleted in the Existing Named Ranges text box
(or click the name of an existing range in the listing).

3. Select the Delete button to delete the name.

or

Select Delete All to delete all previously defined names in
the current worksheet file.

4. Select OK.

NOTES Unless you specify a range explicitly in step 5 of
To Create a Range Name, the range that holds the labels must touch
the selected cell. Use step 5 particularly if you want to define a three-
dimensional range. (See *Ranges*.)

The program will substitute a name you create in any formulas that refer to the range. For a single-cell range address in a formula to be replaced automatically with the name you create here, the address must be expressed as a range. For example, use A1..A1 rather than A1.

Labels must be the same length as range names (1–15 characters).

When you delete a range name, the program replaces it in all formulas with its range address.

To make a range name refer to an absolute (fixed) address, precede the name with a dollar sign ($).

In general, no spaces, punctuation, or special characters are permitted in range names. Avoid names that look like addresses, formulas, keywords, macro commands, etc.

If you use Undefined with a range name that is used in a formula, the result will be displayed as *ERR*.

OPTIONS   In the dialog box in step 4 of *To Create a Range Name*, the For Cells drop-down box appears for the following options, corresponding to the position of the label text in the worksheet in relation to the cell to be named: To The Left, To The Right, Above, or Below. (Be sure to include the cell containing the label in the range you select.)

The Use Labels button can be selected to assign a label to a single-cell range by taking existing label text from adjacent cells. This feature is a convenient shortcut for naming ranges, since labels that define ranges may already exist in the worksheet as captions, column headings, and so on.

SEE ALSO   *Navigator, Protecting Ranges and Files, Ranges, Ranges for Charting, Saving a File*

NAVIGATOR

The Navigator is a button to the left of the formula bar used for jumping to named ranges in the current worksheet file.

To Navigate the Sheet

1. Click the Navigator button. A drop-down list showing all named ranges in the current worksheet file will appear.

2. Click a range name. The pointer will move to the first cell in that range, and the whole range will be highlighted.

 NOTES You will not be able to use the Navigator unless you have named ranges previously with the Range ➤ Name command.

SEE ALSO *Naming a Range, Ranges*

NEW FILE

The command File ➤ New opens a new worksheet file.

New Feature Clicking this SmartIcon creates a new file.

New Feature A list of SmartMasters, or templates for commonly used business forms, will appear when you select File ➤ New or its equivalent. (See notes below.)

To Open a New Worksheet File

1. From the File pull-down menu, select New. A list of SmartMasters will appear.

2. Select a SmartMaster, then select OK.

or

Select OK to accept the default setting: Create A Plain Worksheet.

3. A document window appears. Enter your data.

NOTES If you check the option Skip New File And Welcome Screens in Tools ➤ User Setup, the SmartMaster list will not be displayed in step 2, and a blank worksheet will be created using the default template.

Until you save a file, its name in the title bar will be UNTITLED. If you already have another file open, the name in the title bar will be FILE????.WK4, where ???? is a consecutive number. The file will not exist on disk until you select File ➤ Save or File ➤ Save As.

SEE ALSO *Opening a File, Protecting Ranges and Files, Saving a File, SmartMasters*

NUMBER FORMATTING

The command Style ➤ Number Format sets various parameters that affect the display of the current range and its values. These settings apply to the selected range only and they override the Style ➤ Worksheet Defaults settings.

Automatic

New Feature Multiple currency formats can now be displayed in the same sheet. (See *Currency Formatting*.)

The SmartIcons associated with number formatting are shown in Figure II.12.

To Specify Number Formatting

1. In the current worksheet window, highlight a range to be formatted.

2. From the Style pull-down menu, select Number Format.

3. In the Number Format dialog box, make selections for the option categories: Format, Decimal Places, and Parens (parentheses). (See *Options* below.)

or

To return to format defaults, select Reset.

4. If you wish to redefine your selected range, type a reference in the Range box, or click its button and drag a range in the sheet with the Range Selector pointer.

5. Select OK.

NOTES If you specify a valid Format option that incudes decimals, the Decimal Places option will appear in the dialog box. Its numeric incrementor allows for as many as 15 decimal places.

If you select Reset in step 3, the Style ➤ Worksheet Defaults settings are used.

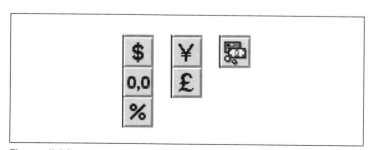

Figure II.12: SmartIcons for number formatting

If you specify a format that is too wide for the corresponding column width, the cell is displayed filled with asterisks (********) instead of the value. (See *Column Width.*)

A Sample box allows you to preview the results of your formatting options.

OPTIONS   Options in the dialog box in step 3 include the following:

Format   The Format options are as follows:

Fixed   Truncates the number of digits to the right of the decimal point to the number you enter in the Decimal Places box.

Scientific   Displays in exponential notation (power of 10).

Currency   Shows with currency sign and decimal point. (See *Currency Formatting.*)

,(Comma)   Shows with thousands separator.

General   Shows numbers without thousands separator (the default).

+/−   In place of the value, shows a horizontal bar graph of plus or minus signs, the number of characters equivalent to the integer, or whole-number, part of the value.

Percent   Displays with a trailing % sign.

Text   Shows formulas as text, numbers as General.

Hidden   Hides; does not display or print.

Automatic   A set of defaults, lets the program determine the format based on the syntax of your entry.

Label   Adds the label prefix (') automatically to any data entered at the formatted address, transforming all entries to text.

Date And Time Formats   Offer a variety of date and time formats, as shown by the examples in the listing.

Parens   Encloses minus values in parentheses ().

Decimal Places   When this option appears, enter a value from 1–15 for the number of digits to appear to the right of the decimal point.

SEE ALSO   *Column Width, Currency Formatting, Protecting Ranges and Files, Worksheet Defaults*

OLE

OLE is an abbreviation of the Windows term *object linking and embedding*, an enhancement and extension of dynamic data exchange (DDE). Lotus 1-2-3 Release 5 for Windows supports OLE 2.0, which not only permits linking of data and embedding of objects between applications, but also supports drag-and-drop copying and moving of data and objects between open application windows.

 SEE ALSO *Linking*

OPENING A FILE

The command File ➤ Open loads an existing worksheet file (.WK4) from disk to become the current worksheet in 1-2-3.

New Feature Use of the Translate Utility to convert foreign files to .WK3 format is no longer required. Such files can be opened directly by using the File ➤ Open command and specifying the file type.

To Open a Worksheet File

1. From the File pull-down menu, select Open (*or* press Ctrl-O).

2. In the dialog box, specify the file in the File name text box. (You can navigate disks and directories through the Files, Directories, and Drives boxes.)

3. Select OK.

4. The contents of the file appear in a new document window in 1-2-3. The pointer is active within the new window.

To Open a Recent File

1. Select File from the menu bar.

2. From the five files listed at the bottom of the File pull-
down menu, select a file name.

NOTES Multiple files can be loaded into 1-2-3 concurrently. Their document windows will overlay one another on the
screen. To move the pointer among windows, you can do any of the
following:

• Click on the title bar of a tiled or cascaded window.

• Click on the tab of the sheet you want.

• Press Ctrl-F6 to cycle through the open document windows.

• Select the worksheet name from the Window pull-down menu.

You can specify that 0–5 of the most recently used file names will be
listed in the File pull-down menu when you select the command
Tools ➤ User Setup.

OPTIONS Several File ➤ Open options are available in
steps 2–4 of "To Open a Worksheet File," above.

File Type Allows you to open or combine the following
file types:

1-2-3.WK* Opens any valid Lotus 1-2-3 spreadsheet.

SmartMaster WT4 Opens 1-2-3 SmartMasters and templates.

Shared NS4 Opens shared files on a Lotus Notes server.

Text Opens text files of the following types: .TXT, .PRN, .CSV,
.DAT, .OUT, and .ASC. For any of these types, the Text Options
button will appear, by which the following options can be set:
Parsing of fields can be by Separator (Tab, Comma, Semicolon,

Space, or Other Character(s)), by Layout Of File, or Put Everything In One Column. The Character Set can be defined as Windows ANSI, DOS or OS/2, Multilingual DOS, Nordic DOS, or US DOS.

Symphony WR*   Opens Lotus Symphony worksheet files.

Excel   Opens Microsoft Excel worksheet files: sheets (.XLS), templates (.XLT), and workbooks (.XLW).

ANSI Metafile   Opens Windows Computer Graphics Metafiles (.CGM files).

1-2-3 Pic   Opens Lotus 1-2-3 Picture files, which contain charts and drawings as vector graphics. (Don't confuse these with some bitmap picture files that also have the .PIC extension.)

dBASE DBF   Opens dBASE and Xbase database files.

Paradox DB   Opens Paradox database files.

All files *.*   Opens any other permitted file type.

Combine

Combines multiple files or ranges in a single worksheet from the above file types. Select one of these options:

Read   Reads into the current worksheet either an Entire File or a Range. Exceptions are Excel files, which cannot be combined with 1-2-3 documents, and text, which is opened as a new worksheet.

Effect In Current File   Determines whether the added data will Replace Values, Add To Values, or Subtract From Values of the open worksheet, as follows:

Replace Values   Copies values from a file to the current sheet. Starting at the current cell, the added data overwrite existing data. Blank cells in the file do not replace values in corresponding cells in the open sheet.

Add To Values   Adds numeric data from a file to values or blank cells in the current sheet. This option adds numbers to existing numbers only. If the incoming value will overlay a label or formula in the open sheet, the incoming value is lost and the current label or formula is retained. Date or time values are not summed; the existing date and time values are retained.

Subtract From Values Subtracts numeric data in a file from numbers or blank cells in the current sheet. Subtracts numbers from other numbers only. If the incoming value will overlay a label or formula in the open sheet, the incoming value is lost and the current label or formula is retained. Dates, times, and positive numbers from blank cells are not subtracted; existing dates, times, and blanks are retained.

 **SEE ALSO** *New File*

PAGE BREAK

The command Style ➤ Page Break controls where new pages will begin when a multipage worksheet file is printed. If Group Mode is on, this command will apply to all worksheets in the file.

To Specify Page Breaks

1. Move the pointer to the leftmost column and top row of the new page.

2. From the Style pull-down menu, select Page Break.

3. In the Page Break dialog box, select Row or Column.

4. Select OK.

NOTES   Page-length settings, which appear as dialog-box options when you select File ➤ Print or File ➤ Page Setup, are overridden by this command, which forces a page break at the location you specify.

A dashed line in the document window indicates a page break.

 SEE ALSO   *Page Setup, Printing, Viewing Preferences*

PAGE SETUP

The command File ➤ Page Setup brings up a dialog box in which you can specify the layout and organization of printed worksheet pages, including headers and footers.

 New Feature   These new SmartIcons are available for controlling the positioning of a worksheet on the printed page.

To Specify Page Setup

1.   From the File pull-down menu, select Page Setup.

2.   In the Page Setup dialog box, type text in the Header and Footer fields, if you wish.

3. Also in the dialog box, change any of the default option set-
    tings to control the look of the page. (See *Options*, below.)

4. Select OK.

NOTES   The Landscape option works only on printers
that support this mode—the program will not rotate the output to
produce Landscape orientation on a Portrait printer. However, this
is a feature of the Allways add-in program.

If you frequently reset the page appearance options, save the settings to a Named Settings layout file. (See *Named Settings*, below.)

OPTIONS   These are the Page Setup options that appear
in the dialog box in steps 2 and 3 above.

Orientation   Select Landscape (long dimension horizontal) or
Portrait (long dimension vertical).

Margins   Enter new margins as measurements on the output
page for the top, bottom, left, and right dimensions. Default settings
are shown for the output format used with the currently installed
printer. Default settings are in inches. To override the measurement
default, after entering the number you can add **mm** for millimeter
or **cm** for centimeter.

Center   Mark one or both check boxes to determine whether the
sheet will be centered Horizontally or Vertically with respect to the
page margins.

Header And Footer   Enter text strings to be printed as headers and footers in left, middle, and right sections at the top and bottom of each page. Leaving these fields blank clears the existing
headers or footers. The Insert button options are Date, Time, Page
Number, File Name, or Cell Contents (provide a cell address). Clicking a Header or Footer field and then a button inserts that item into
the field. The same results can be achieved by typing a prefix in the
field: date (@), time (+), page number (#), file name (^), and cell
contents (\).

Named Settings This option is a shortcut that allows you to Save or Retrieve all the printing options so they can be applied to other worksheets. To save settings in this dialog box to a page-layout library file, select Save and specify the file name. The extension is .AL3.

Size Squeezes or expands, in effect, a worksheet to fit the print area, as defined by the Margins and Borders settings. In the Size drop-down, select one of the following:

Actual Size Prints the area selected in actual text point sizes, starting at the upper-left corner of the printed page.

Fit All To Page Adjusts the degree of compression to fit the Margins and Borders settings.

Fit Columns To Page Adjusts the degree of compression to fit the Margins and Borders settings so that the selected column is on one page.

Fit Rows To Page Adjusts the degree of compression according to the Margins and Borders settings to fit the row on a page.

Manually Scale Reduces or enlarges the worksheet by the percentage you specify. For example, an entry of 150 would enlarge the worksheet 1.5 times. The range is from 15 to 1000%.

SmartIcons for some of these options are shown in Figure II.13.

Show Mark any of the following check boxes to control the appearance of the page (× = on; blank = off).

Worksheet Frame Draws a frame around the page.

Grid Lines Separates columns and rows with grid lines.

Drawn Objects Prints the charts and objects you draw.

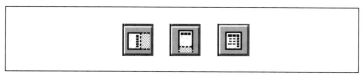

Figure II.13: SmartIcons for sizing data by rows or by columns to fit a page

Print Titles   Provides two options that can improve the look of the printed spreadsheet. Use the selection pointer or type a range reference.

Columns   Lets you select a range that prints as headings for rows, to the left of the data.

Rows   Lets you select a range that prints as headings at the top of each column.

SmartIcons for these options are shown in Figure II.14.

Default Settings   To return options to their default settings, select Restore. To change the defaults to the current, revised settings so that they affect future sessions, select Update.

 **SEE ALSO**   *Headers and Footers, Naming a Range, Previewing Printouts*

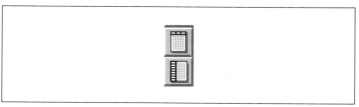

Figure II.14: SmartIcons for setting print titles

PARSING A RANGE

The command Range ➤ Parse can be used after a File ➤ Open ➤ File Type ➤ Text command to convert long labels to multiple columns of data in the current worksheet.

To Parse Long Labels

1. Import text data from an external file into the current worksheet with File ➤ Open ➤ File Type ➤ Text.

2. Move the pointer to a cell that contains a long label.

3. From the Range pull-down menu, select Parse.

4. The Parse dialog box appears. Select the Create button.

5. A new row containing a format line is inserted in the blank area of the initial Parse dialog box. Edit the format line so that each column matches the width and data type of a corresponding string in the long label.

6. In the Parse dialog box, enter the address of the first cell in the first column containing a new format line.

7. In the Output Range text box, enter a range to hold the parsed data.

8. Select OK.

 **NOTES** The parsed data generated by this command overwrites the specified output range.

To clear the range entries so that you can enter new information, select the Reset button in the dialog box, reselect the ranges, then select OK.

If the imported text lines vary in format, select OK after step 5, repeat steps 2–5, and create another format line for the next long label.

SEE ALSO *Column Width, Number Formatting*

PASTING DATA

The command Edit ➤ Paste retrieves data (and possibly formatting) that was previously copied to the Clipboard area by an Edit ➤ Copy or Edit ➤ Cut command in 1-2-3 or another Windows application.

To Paste Data from the Clipboard

1. Place data on the Clipboard with the Edit ➤ Copy or Edit ➤ Cut commands in 1-2-3 or another Windows application.

2. In 1-2-3, open the worksheet file that will receive the data.

3. Highlight the cell or range to which data will be copied.

4. From the Edit pull-down menu, select Paste.

or

Press Ctrl-V or Shift-Ins.

NOTES   When a formula is copied to addresses that differ from those in the source file, the program updates the addresses, provided that the references are relative (the default) or mixed. The $ syntax can be used in addresses to specify that an address is absolute and cannot be changed. (See *Ranges*.)

Edit ➤ Paste can be performed repeatedly to retrieve multiple copies of the same source data, such as when you wish to place the data in different sheets in a three-dimensional file. Copied data is retained on the Clipboard until you perform a second Edit ➤ Copy or Edit ➤ Cut command, either in 1-2-3 or in another Windows program. The Clipboard can be used to move data among 1-2-3 worksheets or among different applications in Windows.

To establish DDE links between Windows files, use Edit ➤ Paste Link instead. To embed an OLE object, use Edit ➤ Insert Object.

SEE ALSO *Cutting Data to the Clipboard, Inserting Objects, Linking, Opening a File, Pasting Linked Data, Saving a File*

PASTING FORMATS AND OBJECTS

The command Edit ➤ Paste Special copies styles, converts formulas to values, copies the results of a formula without copying the formula, or embeds an existing object. Edit ➤ Paste Special is also used when linking from another application to 1-2-3. Using Edit ➤ Paste Special instead of Edit ➤ Paste gives you more control over the appearance of the linked data by letting you select the format.

 This SmartIcon pastes cell styles.

 This one pastes formulas as values.

To Copy Data and Selected Attributes

1. Select the data to be copied, and place it in the Clipboard using Edit ➤ Copy.

2. Select Edit from the menu bar.

3. Select Paste ➤ Special from the Edit pull-down menu.

4. In the Paste Special dialog box, select the format of the data being pasted. Choices include All, Cell Contents Only, Styles Only, or Formulas As Values.

5. Select OK.

To Paste and Link Special Data and Formats

1. Place data on the Clipboard with the Edit ➤ Copy or Edit ➤ Cut commands in 1-2-3 or another Windows application.

2. In 1-2-3, open the worksheet file that will receive the data.

3. Highlight the cell or range to which data will be copied.

4. From the Edit pull-down menu, select Paste Special.

5. Select a format from the Using Clipboard Format list. The Paste Special dialog box will display the formats shared between 1-2-3 and the server application.

6. Select Paste to insert, or Paste Link to insert and link.

SEE ALSO *Copying Data to the Clipboard, Inserting Objects, Linking, Pasting Data, Pasting Linked Data*

PASTING LINKED DATA

The command Edit ➤ Paste Link copies data and formatting from the Clipboard to the current worksheet and also establishes a link to the source file from which the data was extracted. You can then perform Dynamic Data Exchange (DDE) among active Windows documents and applications. Changing the data in one application and file will change it in all the other active files to which it is linked.

To Paste Data and Link Files

1. Place data on the Clipboard with the Edit ➤ Copy or Edit ➤ Cut commands in 1-2-3 or another Windows application.

2. In 1-2-3, open the worksheet file that will receive the data.

3. Highlight the cell or range to which data will be copied.

4. From the Edit pull-down menu, select Paste Link.

NOTES If you are unable to establish a link using this command, use Edit ➤ Links ➤ Create and specify a DDE/OLE link.

All links to the current worksheet can be viewed in a list box by selecting Edit ➤ Links.

Formatting copied with Edit ➤ Paste includes settings made through the Style menu, such as Font and Color.

SEE ALSO *Copying Data to the Clipboard, Cutting Data to the Clipboard, Inserting Objects, Linking, Opening a File, Pasting Data, Saving a File*

PREFERRED CHART TYPE

The command Chart ➤ Set Preferred permits you to change the options in an existing default chart to your preselected preferences. You can then apply these options by the command Chart ➤ Use Preferred.

CHART ➤ SET PREFERRED

This command copies the option settings of the current chart to serve as a template for new charts.

To Record the Attributes of the Current Chart

1. Select a chart by clicking on it. (Small square handles should surround the entire chart area.)

2. From the menu bar, select Chart Type. Change the chart to your desired Chart Type and set the options. (See *Chart Type.*) Select OK.

3. From the Chart menu, select Set Preferred.

NOTES This command does not change the default options when you create a chart by selecting a data range and selecting Tools ➤ Chart. However, the Chart ➤ Use Preferred command is a quick way to apply your preferences to such a chart.

CHART ➤ USE PREFERRED

This command applies the options you set previously with Chart ➤ Set Preferred.

To Apply Preferred Options

1. Select a chart by clicking on it. (Small square handles should surround the entire chart area.)

2. From the Chart pull-down, select Use Preferred.

NOTES You must create a default chart first. Select the data range(s) and choose Tools ➤ Chart. The chart will be plotted automatically with default options. Then do steps 1 and 2 above to customize the chart.

 **SEE ALSO** *Charting, Chart Types*

PREVIEWING PRINTOUTS

The command File ➤ Print Preview displays a simulation of printed
worksheet outputs on your computer screen. If included in
the worksheet, margins, frames, grids, styles (such as
graphics), and attributes (such as fonts) will be shown—
sized and positioned correctly in relation to the output page.

New Feature   Preview mode now permits you to view multiple sheets in the current file as they would be printed on a single page.

To Preview Printed Pages

1.   Optionally, highlight the ranges in the current worksheet
that you want to print.

2.   From the File pull-down menu, select Print Preview.

3.   In the Print Preview dialog box, you can specify one or
more print ranges in the Range(s) text box. Use semicolons (;) to separate multiple range addresses or names.

4.   Also in the dialog box, specify which pages are to be
previewed.

5.   If you wish to change the appearance of the page before
you preview it, select the Page Setup button and reset the
File ➤ Page Setup dialog box. (See *Page Setup.*)

6.   Select OK.

7.   The first printed page appears on the screen. To cycle
through multiple pages, press Esc, Page Up, or Page
Down repeatedly (*or* click the page-control buttons on the
screen).

8.   When you have viewed the last page, press Esc to return
to the worksheet document window.

 **NOTES**   Selecting the Page Setup button in step 5 is the same as executing the File ➤ Page Setup command and takes you to a dialog box for entry of the header and footer, as well as options for the layout and appearance of the printed page. See the *Options* section of the entry *Page Setup*.

 **OPTIONS**   In step 4, you can specify the following options:

Preview   Select whether to view the Current Worksheet only, All Worksheets in the file (combined on the page, if they will fit), or a Selected Range.

Pages   To print part of a file, enter the starting page in the From Page text box and the ending page in the To box. To re-number the pages in the print range, enter the first page number in the Starting Page Number box. These settings determine the pages that will appear in Preview mode. This page selection can be overridden in the Print dialog box.

SEE ALSO   *Page Setup*

PRINTER SETUP

The command File ➤ Printer Setup permits you to change options for any printer that has already been installed on your computer through the Windows Control Panel.

To Set Printer Options

1.   From the File pull-down menu, select Printer Setup.

2.   In the Printer Setup dialog box, select the printer name in the Printers list box.

3. To accept the default options for the printer you've selected, select OK.

or

To change the options, select the Setup button.

4. If you chose Setup, a dialog box containing options for the
installed printer appears. Reset the options and select OK.
(See *Options*, below.)

5. Select OK to close the Printer Setup dialog box.

NOTES Printers shown in the list box in step 2 must have
been installed previously through the Windows Program Manager
Control Panel. When you change settings with this command,
you're actually making the changes in Program Manager.

To install a different printer, exit to Program Manager and select
Add Printer from the Printers dialog box of the Control Panel
(found in the Main program group).

OPTIONS Options in the <printer name> dialog box in
step 4 will vary among the printer driver families, or subgroups, by
make and model. Typical options include the following:

Resolution Typical options for the number of dots per inch
(dpi) on a printed page include High (600 or 300 dpi), Me-
dium, and Low (usually 75 dpi).

Paper Source The options available may include Manual
feed, Tractor feed, and Sheet feed (Bin 1 or Bin 2).

Orientation Select Landscape (long dimension horizontal) or
Portrait (long dimension vertical).

Paper Size Select among the paper sizes your printer supports, which can include Letter, Legal, Wide (11×14 inches), A4
(European letter size), Fanfold, and A3 (another European size).

Fonts If the printer supports multiple resident fonts, select
the Font button in the dialog box and then select the desired
font(s) from the Font Options list box. Otherwise, Windows
TrueType fonts will be sent to the printer as graphics.

SEE ALSO   *Page Setup, Previewing Printouts, Printing*

PRINTING

The command File ➤ Print outputs the current worksheet file to the printer.

New Feature   This new SmartIcon prints the current worksheet with default settings, bypassing the usual dialog boxes.

Other SmartIcons for printing are shown in Figure II.15.

To Print a File

1. Highlight the ranges in the current worksheet that you want to print. (See *Options*, below.)

2. From the File pull-down menu, select Print (*or* press Ctrl-P).

3. In the Print dialog box, you can specify one or more print ranges in the range(s) text box. Use semicolons (;) to separate multiple range addresses or names.

4. Also in the dialog box, specify which pages are to be printed.

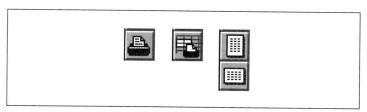

Figure II.15: SmartIcons for setting print titles

5. If you wish to change the appearance of the page before you print it, select the Page Setup button and reset the Page Setup dialog box. (See *Page Setup*.)

6. Before printing, to see how pages will look, select the Preview button. (See *Previewing Printouts*.)

7. Select OK.

NOTES   In the Print dialog box in step 5, selecting Page Setup is the same as selecting File ➤ Page Setup, presenting you with a dialog box for headers, footers, and page appearance options. Selecting Preview is the same as executing File ➤ Print Preview, displaying an on-screen simulation of each page in the print range.

If a print range has a long label, include the overlapped cells as well as the cell that holds the label in steps 1 and 3.

OPTIONS   In step 4, specify in the Number Of Copies text box how many times the file is to be printed. Also specify the starting page in the From Page text box and the ending page in the To box. To renumber the pages in the print range, enter the first page number in the Starting Page Number box.

The Print dialog box has the following options:

Print   Allows you to select the Current Worksheet, All Worksheets, or a Selected Range.

Pages   Allows you to select the pages to print. From Page allows you to select the page number (1–9999) at which printing will begin. This is useful when printing multiple sections of a report.

Number Of Copies   Allows you to print from 1–9999 copies.

 **SEE ALSO**   *Page Setup, Previewing Printouts*

PROTECTING RANGES AND FILES

The command Style ➤ Protection can be used to change the protection status of a range, which only becomes operative after you have used File ➤ Protect to seal the file.

STYLE ➤ PROTECTION

This command permits you to allow changes in cell contents in a range after you have sealed the file using File ➤ Protect. You must use Style ➤ Protection to unprotect cells explicitly before you seal a file.

To Protect or Unprotect a Range

1. In the current worksheet window, highlight a range for which protection status will be changed.

2. From the Style pull-down menu, mark the check box Keep Data Unprotected After File Is Sealed to permit changes to the cells; unmark the box to protect the cells.

3. If you did not select a range in step 1, or if you wish to re-define your selected range, type a reference in the Range box, or click its button and drag a range in the sheet with the Range Selector pointer.

4. Select OK.

5. Seal the file using File ➤ Protect.

NOTES   All worksheet cells have the protected style attributed by default, but protection is activated only when you seal a file with File ➤ Protect. You therefore use the Style ➤ Protection command only to *remove* protection and to permit changes in specific ranges within file that you intend to seal.

The symbol *Pr* appears in the status bar when you select a protected cell, *U* for an explicitly unprotected cell. (The text color is also different for all unprotected cells.)

To unprotect cell contents in a sealed file, first select File ➤ Protect again to remove the seal. Select Style ➤ Protection as described above to unprotect specific cells, marking the check box in step 2. Reseal the file using File ➤ Protect.

This type of protection does not apply to drawn objects, which can be *locked* by the command Edit ➤ Arrange ➤ Lock.

FILE ➤ PROTECT

This command permits three different ways to control file sharing on network or multi-user systems. First, a *seal* can lock out other users from making changes to the worksheet. Second, a *reservation,* a type of file lock, can prevent access to a worksheet file while the user with the reservation is working on that file. At your option, the first user who retrieves the file will have the reservation automatically for the duration of the session. Third, a *password,* or access code, can limit those who can access your worksheets.

To Seal a File

1. From the File pull-down menu, select Protect.

2. In the Protect dialog box, under File Protection, mark the Seal File check box.

3. Select OK.

4. In the Set Password dialog box, type a password once in the Password text box, press Tab, type it again in the Verify password text box, and select OK.

To Remove or Change a Seal Password

1. From the File pull-down menu, select Protect.

2. In the Protect dialog box, under File Protection, unmark the Seal File check box.

3. Select OK.

4. In the Set Password dialog box, enter the current password.

5. Select OK.

6. Optionally, to create a new password, repeat the steps to seal a file (see above, "To Seal a File"). Specify a new password when 1-2-3 prompts you for it.

To Get a Reservation

1. From the File pull-down menu, select Protect.

2. Under File Reservation, select Get.

3. Select OK.

To Release a Reservation

1. From the File pull-down menu, select Protect.

2. Under File Reservation, select Release.

3. Select OK.

To Turn Automatic Reservation On and Off

1. From the File pull-down menu, select Protect.

2. Mark the Get Reservation Automatically check box.

3. Select OK.

NOTES   Sealing a file prevents changes to cell contents, styles, and settings. Other users can still change data in any range that was *unprotected* when you sealed the file. All cells are protected by default, the protection being activated when the file is sealed. To unprotect a cell or range, select it and select Style ➤ Protection, mark the Keep Data Unprotected check box, and select OK.

In order to hold the reservation for the current file, two conditions must be true: the file must be available, and no one can have saved the file since you read it into memory. When you get the reservation, you are the only person who can save changes to the file.

With automatic reservation, the first user who reads the file into memory gets the file reservation lock. The file reservation is automatically released when the user closes the file.

Before you release the reservation, be sure you use File ➤ Save if you want to save changes you made to the file.

The status bar displays *Pr* when a protected cell is selected and *U* for an unprotected cell.

While a file is sealed, you cannot do any of the following:

• Change the file reservation setting.

• Use the commands Style, Tools ➤ Chart, Tools ➤ Draw, Tools ➤ Database ➤ New Query, or Tools ➤ Map.

• Use certain Edit, View, Tools, and Range commands.

• Name or rename worksheets or worksheet tabs.

• Enter data in ranges that have not been unprotected with the Style ➤ Protection command.

 **SEE ALSO** *Locking Objects, Saving a File*

QUERYING DATABASES

Applies to a set of commands for finding data items in 1-2-3 *database tables* and extracting them to a separate *query table*. The definitions are:

Database table   Is a range that contains one column for each field of a typical database record, ordered from left to right in the order the fields appear in the database records. The top row in the table contains column-heading labels that are used as field names. Column widths correspond to field lengths, and cell formatting controls data typing.

Query table   Is a working copy of a database table in which fields and records may be reordered or recalculated.

Having created a database table, you can start a new query, extracting results to a separate table, by the command Tools ➤ Database ➤ New Query.

Once a query table has been selected, the commands Query ➤ Set Database Table, Query ➤ Set Options, and Query ➤ Show SQL become available.

TOOLS ➤ DATABASE ➤ NEW QUERY

 This command permits you to initiate various operations on a database table by extracting a separate query table.

To Query Database Tables

1.   From the Tools pull-down menu, select Database.

2.   From the Database cascade menu, select New Query. The New Query dialog box will appear.

3.   Specify the range containing the database table(s) from which a new query table will be extracted: Type a reference in the Select A Database To Query box, or click its button and use the Range Selector pointer to drag a range in the sheet.

   or

   Select the External button to connect to an external database. (See *External Databases*.)

4.   Select the fields and their order using the Choose Fields button. (See *Choosing Fields for a Query*.)

5.   Select the options for filtering records by using the Set Criteria button. (See *Criteria for Queries*.)

6. Specify a blank range in the current sheet to hold the new query table: Type a reference in the Select Location For A New Query Table box or click its button to use the Range Selector pointer.

7. Select OK.

NOTES   You can query an external table as the input range to this command if you have first connected to the database system through Tools ➤ Database ➤ Connect To External.

To access multiple database tables, enter table names separated by commas in the input range text box in step 3.

OPTIONS   In the Set Criteria dialog box, select from the following options:

And Limits the records to find by adding another criterion.

Or Expands the number of records to find with an alternative criterion.

Clear Resets the entries in the Field, Operator, Value, and Criteria Range text boxes so that you can enter new information for another query operation.

Refresh Automatically updates both the query and the records in the database table.

Limit Records This option limits the number of records that are returned in a query. Complex queries can run a long time (and possibly cause memory overflows) if the database is very large, if the logical operators are wrong, or if multiple criteria are specified. To improve performance, set the limit to a smaller number. The default limit when you are connected to an external database is 25 records.

QUERY ➤ SET DATABASE TABLE

This command lets you query a different database table.

To Query a Different Database Table

1. Select a query table. A bold border and handles should surround the table, and the Query selection should appear in the menu bar.

2. From the Query pull-down menu, select Set Database Table.

3. Select the range that contains the database table

or

Press F3. The Database Name dialog box appears. Select a table from the Database Names list box.

4. Select OK.

NOTES If the new database table matches all the fields in the current table, this command selects the new database table with the same options you selected for the current one. These optional settings include Criteria, Sort, Aggregates, and Range Address of the query table. If the fields do not match, the Criteria, Sort, Aggregates, and Join settings are cleared.

To specify an external database table, select the External button. You can also name the external table with a range name.

QUERY ➤ SET OPTIONS

This command specifies options for manipulating data in database and query tables.

To Set Query Options

1. Select a query table. A bold border and handles should surround the table, and the Query selection should appear in the menu bar.

2. From the Query pull-down menu, select Set Options.

3. Mark the check boxes for the options you want. (See *Options* below.)

4. Select OK.

OPTIONS The dialog box in step 3 includes the following:

Allow Updates To Database Table Posts any changes made in the query table to the database table, as well. The default is off, which prevents accidental corruption of the database.

Show Unique Records Only Excludes duplicate records from the results of queries.

Show Sample Values In Filters Displays values for the criteria in a query table. For very large database tables, especially those on network servers, performance will be improved by unmarking this option.

Auto Refresh Updates the query table results automatically when you change any option or entry. Options include Criteria, Sort settings, Field Names, or Aggregate selections. For very large database tables, and especially those on network servers, performance will be improved by unmarking this option. When this option is unmarked, use Query ➤ Refresh Now to update the query table.

SEE ALSO *Criteria for Queries, Databases, External Databases, Updating a Database Query*

QUICK MENUS

Quick menus are lists of shortcut commands that pop up when you point to a data item or object with the mouse and click the *right* mouse button. Select an item in any quick menu by moving the highlight to it and pressing *either* mouse button.

OPTIONS The selections in a quick menu depend on the type of object selected and the commands that are valid for that object.

Selections As an example, if you select a worksheet range and then click the right mouse button, the quick menu that pops up will contain the following selections: (Edit) Cut, (Edit) Copy, (Edit) Paste, (Edit) Clear, (Edit) Copy Down, (Edit) Copy Right, (Range) Fill By Example, (Style) Number Format, (Style) Font & Attributes, (Style) Lines & Color, (Style) Alignment, and (Range) Name.

Object types Selected objects for which quick menus appear include cells and ranges, charts, objects within charts (such as bars and grid lines), drawn objects, and query tables.

 **SEE ALSO** *Keyboard Shortcuts, SmartIcons*

RANGES

Ranges are rectangular blocks of contiguous cells. A range can be specified by two cell *addresses*: the cell in its upper-left corner (see Figure II.16) and the cell in its lower-right corner. If the range includes only a single column, its boundaries are the top and bottom cells. If the range includes just one row, its boundaries are the cells at its left and right ends. A range can also be a single cell, in which case its address is simply the cell address.

To Key in a Range Address

1. When you see a text box labeled Range within a dialog box, click on the text box to activate its cursor. Or, press Tab repeatedly until the box is highlighted.

2. Type the range address, using the syntax W:Am..X:Zn. (See *Notes*, below.)

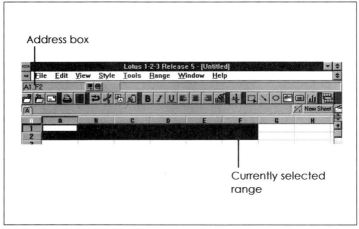

Address box

Currently selected range

Figure II.16: The selection indicator near the upper-left corner of the 1-2-3 screen shows the address or name of the current location of the pointer.

To Specify a Range with the Mouse

1. Move the pointer to the worksheet that contains the range to be selected.

2. Move the pointer to the cell in the first (upper-left) corner in the range.

3. Drag the pointer to the opposite corner and release. The entire range should now be highlighted.

To Specify a Range by Name

1. Drag the pointer to highlight the desired range.

2. Use the Range ➤ Name command to assign a name to the range you have specified.

3. Whenever the program prompts you for a range address (as in a text box labeled Range), simply type the name instead.

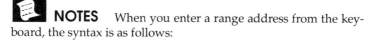 **NOTES** When you enter a range address from the keyboard, the syntax is as follows:

W Letter of the top worksheet in a three-dimensional range (optional).

A Column letter of the cell in the first (upper-left) corner.

m Row number of the cell in the first corner.

X Letter of the bottom worksheet in a three-dimensional range (optional).

Z Column letter of the cell in the second (lower-right) corner.

n Row number of the second corner.

The W and X parameters are used for specifying three-dimensional ranges, which can span multiple sheets in the same file. The worksheet letter must be separated from the cell address by a colon (:). To specify a range within the current worksheet, you may omit *both* worksheet letters from the syntax. That is, Am..Zn is interpreted as a range in the current worksheet. In any range address, the first and second cell addresses must be separated by the double-period (..) symbol and must not contain any spaces (blanks).

The W parameters in the current file appear as *worksheet tabs* above the document window. Click a tab to select its sheet. Optionally, you can rename the sheets by double-clicking on a tab and typing a new sheet name.

OPTIONS In 1-2-3, references to cell addresses normally are adjusted when columns, rows, or ranges are inserted or deleted. However, syntax options make it possible to control the ways in which addresses are adjusted.

Relative By default, addresses are relative; they are adjusted by the program automatically. Addresses that can be changed include references in formulas and range name definitions. To specify relative addressing, simply use the syntax described above.

Absolute Any element of a range or cell address (sheet letter, column letter, and/or row number) can be specified as *absolute*, or fixed, by preceding it with a dollar sign ($) in the address syntax. Examples include $A$1, $A$1..$ZZ$99, and $A:$A$1..$ZZ:$ZZ$99.

Mixed   In some circumstances, it might be necessary to specify one corner of a range as fixed and the other as relative. Thus, a range address can be mixed, or include both relative and absolute references. Examples include A$1 (column relative, row absolute) $A$1..Z99 (first corner absolute, second corner relative).

 **SEE ALSO**   *Naming a Range*

RANGES FOR CHARTING

The command Chart ➤ Ranges lets you assign worksheet ranges to the X axis and chart data series A–W of an existing chart. Optionally, you can specify that any of the chart data ranges will be plotted against a second Y (2nd Y) axis. You can also specify that any of the chart data ranges be represented by a different type of chart, making a mixed chart. Chart data ranges can also be defined by Column, by Row, or Individually based on ranges in the worksheet.

To Reassign Data Ranges for Charting

1.   Select a chart by clicking on it. (Small square handles should surround the entire chart area.)

2.   From the Chart pull-down menu, select Ranges.

or

Click the right mouse button to activate a quick menu and select Chart ➤ Ranges.

3.   To assign ranges Individually, in the Chart Ranges dialog box, enter the addresses or names of ranges in the Series box for the X data range (usually the axis labels) and data series A–W.

or

To use a worksheet range you have set up especially for charting, select By Row or By Column from the Assign Ranges drop-down box. Skip step 4. (See *Notes* below.)

4. Optionally, to plot any of the chart data ranges against a second Y axis, select the 2nd Y check box.

5. To change the plotting style of the selected data series, select a new Type from the Mixed drop-down box.

6. Select OK.

 **NOTES**   If you use the By Row or By Column methods of assigning data ranges in step 3, the worksheet range must be set up specially for charting. Data ranges must correspond either to consecutive rows or to consecutive columns in the worksheet.

For example, the first row or column will be assigned to the X data series. Rows or columns 2–23 will be assigned in sequence to data series A–W. If you specify a range that has only one row or column, the program makes it data series A.

When you assign ranges By Row or By Column order, a sample worksheet graphic appears in the dialog box to show you how to set up the data range, the x-axis labels, and the legend. When you click the button on the right end of the Range box, a selection pointer icon appears with which you can select a range in the sheet (see Figure II.17).

If you select Pie as the chart type, the first column will be used as pie-slice labels (data series X), and the second column (or row) will be data series A. A single pie chart has only one data series. However, data series B can be used to assign colors and explosion options to pie slices. The color number held in each cell in this range will be assigned to the corresponding slice of the pie (see Figure II.18).

SEE ALSO   *Chart Types, Naming a Range*

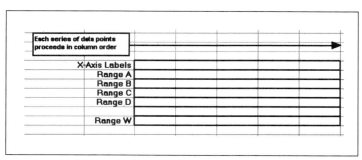

Figure II.17: Worksheet layout for assignment of Chart Ranges, by row. Ranges can also be assigned by column. For most chart types, except pies, Release 5 permits data ranges A–W.

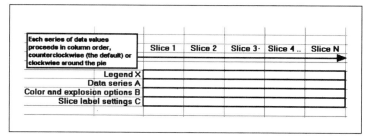

Figure II.18: Worksheet layout for pie chart data, by row. Ranges can also be assigned by column.

REGRESSION ANALYSIS

The command Range ➤ Analyze ➤ Regression performs multiple linear *regression analysis* to find any linear correlation between two sets of data or ranges. The first set, or *X range*, is the independent variable, and the second set, or *Y range*, is the dependent variable.

For example, in a set of experimental data, the independent variable is a set of given values, and the dependent variable is the output from an equation or model. Statistics from the comparison are placed in the *output range* you specify. A best-fit straight line of X-Y points is calculated to determine the *slope*, or trend, of the data.

To Perform Regression Analysis

1. From the Range pull-down menu, select Analyze.

2. From the Analyze cascade menu, select Regression.

3. The Regression dialog box appears. In the X range text box, enter the range containing the X values, or the independent variables.

4. In the Y-range text box, enter the range containing the Y values, or the dependent variables.

5. In the Output range text box, enter the range to hold the calculated results. (The address of the first cell is sufficient.)

6. For the Y intercept, select one of the option buttons, Compute or Set To Zero.

7. To enter new ranges in steps 3–5 and options, select Reset and repeat those steps.

8. Select OK.

NOTES The results generated by this command overwrite the cells in the output range.

The maximum number of columns in the X range is 75. These must be adjacent to one another. The Y range must be in one column with the same number of rows as the X range.

Results placed in the output range include the following:

Y-Axis Intercept A numeric value

Degrees Of Freedom Number of observations – number of X values – 1

Number Of Observations Number of rows in X and Y ranges

R^2 **Value** The reliability of the analysis. Values closer to 1 indicate a stronger correlation.

Standard Error Of the X coefficients

Standard Error Of the Y estimate

X Coefficients Slope for each X variable

 **OPTIONS** In step 6, select one of the following option buttons for the Y-Intercept option:

Compute Automatically calculates the Y-axis intercept, or the point at which the regression line (trend) intersects the Y axis.

Set To Zero Causes 1-2-3 to use zero as the Y-axis intercept. (This is true only if zero values in the X range would result in zeros in the Y range. If you set this incorrectly, the R^2 value will be negative, which is an error.) Do not select this option unless your data is such that if all the independent variables equaled zero, the dependent variable would also equal zero.

 SEE ALSO *Backsolver, Distribution Analysis, Solver, What-If Tables*

RENAMING A FILE

Renaming a file can be done for the current worksheet by performing File ➤ Save As and typing a different file name.

 SEE ALSO *Saving a File*

REPORT GENERATION

 The command Tools ➤ Database ➤ Report starts the Lotus Approach application in which you can generate a report from a 1-2-3 database table.

This command requires installation of Lotus Approach 3.0 or higher on the same system.

To Generate a Report from a 1-2-3 Database

1. In 1-2-3, select the database table.

2. From the menu bar, select Tools ➤ Database ➤ Report. A message box will appear.

3. Select OK. Approach will start, and its Form Assistant will open, permitting access to the selected 1-2-3 database table.

4. Use Approach commands to manipulate records in the database and generate the report. (Click the ? button or press F1 for help on procedures in Approach.)

5. When you are finished working with the report, from the Approach menu bar, select File ➤ Exit And Return. Approach will terminate and you will be returned 1-2-3.

or

From the Approach menu bar, select File ➤ Close And Return. The Approach application will remain open but inactive, and you will be returned to 1-2-3.

The Approach report will be embedded in the 1-2-3 sheet as an OLE button.

6. In 1-2-3, select File ➤ Save or File ➤ Save As to save both the worksheet and the embedded Approach report in the same .WK4 file.

 **NOTES** Double-click the embedded button in 1-2-3 to restart Approach. If the records in the database have changed since you last opened the form, the report will be updated automatically.

Approach permits only 256 characters in a database field, but 512 are permitted in 1-2-3. Approach will use only the first 256 characters of each text item.

SEE ALSO *Databases, Querying Databases*

ROTATING OBJECTS

The command Edit ➤ Arrange ➤ Rotate lets you to rotate an object up to 360 degrees around its center.

To Rotate an Object

1. Select the object you want to rotate.

2. From the Edit pull-down menu, select Arrange.

3. From the cascade menu, select Rotate.

4. Move the mouse pointer to rotate the object.

5. Double-click the left mouse button to indicate the new position of the object.

 **NOTES**   When Rotate is selected, the mouse pointer will change to a cross at the end of an axis line that runs through the center of the selected object.

Objects can be selected and rotated independently of each other, or the Select All Objects icon can be used to rotate all objects equally at the same time.

The SmartIcon for rotating text in a range places each line of text at a 45-degree angle, which can be useful for arranging headings in narrow columns.

SEE ALSO   *Arranging Objects, Flipping Objects, Selecting Data and Objects*

ROW HEIGHT

The command Style ➤ Row Height sets the height of rows in terms of the point size of the current font. Optionally, you can reset row height to the default size.

To Set Row Height

1. In the current worksheet window, highlight a range of rows to be adjusted.

   or

   With the mouse, move the pointer to the row-number area and then drag the bottom border of a row to adjust the row height. Skip the rest of these steps. (The program must be in Ready mode.)

2. From the Style pull-down menu, select Row Height.

3. In the Row Height dialog box, select Set Height To and enter the height in points (1–255) in the text box.

or

Select Fit Largest Font to select the largest text size in the data automatically.

4. If you wish to redefine your selected range, type a reference in the Range box, or click its button and drag a range in the sheet with the Range Selector pointer.

5. Select OK.

NOTES Regardless of the settings you make here, the program will adjust row height to fit the largest font specified in that row. To reduce the row height, it may also be necessary to reset font size with Style Font & Attributes.

SEE ALSO *Column Width, Fonts and Attributes*

SAVING A FILE

You can save a file by using the commands File ➤ Save or File ➤ Save As.

FILE ➤ SAVE

The command File ➤ Save writes the current worksheet to disk with the file name shown in the title bar of the worksheet's document window. (If a new sheet is UNTITLED or FILE*.WK4, the Save As dialog box will appear and you can type a new file name.)

To Save a File

1. Select the document window of the worksheet you want to save.

2. From the File pull-down menu, select Save (*or* press Ctrl-S).

3. If the Save As dialog box appears, type a new file name or accept the default file name, and select OK.

NOTES The program will warn you if this command will overwrite an existing file.

The Save As dialog box will appear if you are saving a new file for the first time. The program automatically assigns a name to an UN-TITLED file. The default name is *FILEnnnn.WK4*, where *nnnn* is the next consecutive number for a new sheet. To change the default name of a new file, type over it in the File Name text box or save an existing file with File ➤ Save As instead. If you wish, you can also assign a password to the file during the operation by marking the Save With Password check box.

FILE ➤ SAVE AS

This command permits you to rename the current worksheet file as it is saved to disk. You can also specify password protection for the new file.

Optionally, you can save a selected range, including formulas and values, or values only, in a worksheet file (.WK*) on disk. This command option does not copy drawn objects or styles, except for number formats and alignments.

To Rename and Save a File

1. Select the document window of the worksheet you want to save.

2. From the File pull-down menu, select Save As.

3. In the Save As dialog box, type the new file name in the File Name text box. (You can navigate disks and directories through the Files, Directories, and Drives boxes.)

4. Also in the dialog box, mark the Save With Password check box if you wish to restrict access to the file.

5. Select OK.

6. If you selected Save With Password, type the password, press Tab, retype it, then select OK.

To Save a Selected Range Only

1. Highlight the range.

2. From the File pull-down menu, select Save As.

3. Type a file name. The default extension is .WK4. To specify a text file, select the extension .TXT in the File Name text box or in the File Type drop-down box pick .TXT.

4. Mark the Selected Range Only check box.

5. Select OK.

6. In step 3, if you selected a worksheet file (.WK*), a Save Range As dialog box appears. Select Formulas And Values or Values Only.

7. Select OK.

NOTES To save the current worksheet file without renaming it, use File ➤ Save instead. The file name is shown in the title bar of its document window.

If you specify an existing file, the program prompts you to cancel the command, replace the data, or create a backup of the file before overwriting its data. Backup files have the same name as the worksheets, but with the extension .BAK.

 **SEE ALSO** *New File, Opening a File*

SELECTING DATA AND OBJECTS

Data items in cells and objects must be selected before they can be manipulated or changed by commands. An object that has been selected is surrounded by *handles*, or small squares. Also, multiple objects can be selected in a single operation so that a command can be performed on them as a group.

Multiple objects in a selection are called a *collection*. Multiple objects that have been combined to form a single object constitute a *group*.

> **New Feature**   Charting, editing, application of styles, printing, SmartSum, and fill-by-example operations can now be performed on collections.

The three SmartIcons associated with object selection are shown in Figure II.19.

To Select One Object with the Mouse

1.   Move the pointer to the edge of the object and click on it.

2.   Handles appear around the object. If the handles appear around another object nearby instead, move the pointer and click again.

3.   Repeat step 2 until handles appear around the object you want.

Figure II.19: SmartIcons for object selection

To Select Several Objects at Once

1. Click the Select Several Objects SmartIcon. The pointer will change to a small crosshairs.

or

 Hold down Ctrl or Shift as you click the edge of each object to be selected, and skip the rest of these steps.

2. Drag a box that completely surrounds the objects to be selected, touching none of them.

3. Handles should appear around all objects that were contained in the box.

To Release Selected Objects

• Move the pointer off the objects and click.

To Release One of a Group of Selected Objects

• Move the pointer to the object and click on it while pressing Ctrl or Shift.

To Select Cells and Ranges

1. Click on a cell to select it. The cell will be highlighted and its address and contents will appear in boxes in the top-left corner of the screen.

or

To select a range, click on a cell in one corner of the range and drag the pointer to the opposite corner. The range will be highlighted.

2. To include other, nonadjacent cells, hold down the Ctrl key as you click each cell or drag each range to be added to the collection.

3. If the collection must include items in other open sheets, click the worksheet tab to activate the sheet and continue adding to the collection (step 2).

To Scroll the Display

• Drag the slider (square bar) in the scroll box until the display is adjusted to suit you.

   or

• To scroll the display one line or increment at a time, click on either of the arrow buttons at the ends of the scroll box. Repeat until the display is adjusted to suit you.

To Use the Range Selector in a Dialog Box

1. Move the pointer to the Range text box and click on the Range Selector button. The dialog box will disappear and the pointer will change to the Range Selector.

2. Drag the Range Selector pointer in the sheet to select a range. When you release the mouse button, the dialog box reappears and the range is entered in the text box.

NOTES   To select objects with the keyboard, use the Edit ➤ Go To or Edit ➤ Arrange commands. These commands can also be performed with the mouse.

You can also select ranges by holding down the Shift key and scrolling with the arrow keys.

Nonadjacent ranges that are included in the same selection are treated as a collection.

Objects within Charts cannot be ungrouped (Edit ➤ Arrange ➤ Ungroup).

When an object has been selected successfully, handles (small squares) appear around it. You can resize some types of objects by dragging a handle. Corner handles allow you to increase both the height and width of an object. Top and bottom horizontal mid-point handles allow you to increase the height of an object. Vertical mid-point handles allow you to increase the width of an object. (An example of an object that cannot be resized vertically is a set of bars in a bar chart.)

If its handles are in the shape of diamonds instead of squares, the object is locked, or protected from modification. You must use Edit ➤ Arrange ➤ Unlock before you can make changes.

You can move some types of objects by dragging them when they are surrounded by handles.

You can also change the attributes of selected objects by executing commands included in the Edit ➤ Arrange cascade and Style pull-down menus.

Objects are created in a succession of layers. The object created first is on the lowest layer, or is farthest back. Objects on top (or in front) obscure those beneath where they overlap. To change the order and thus the way objects overlay one another, use Edit ➤ Arrange commands. The Edit ➤ Arrange commands are particularly useful for sorting out multiple object copies that have been superimposed on one another by previous Edit ➤ Paste operations.

Clicking the right mouse button when an object is selected will cause a quick menu to pop up containing the commands for modifying objects of that type.

 **SEE ALSO** *Arranging Objects, Go To, Grouping Objects, Moving Objects, Quick Menus*

SENDING MAIL

Mail can be sent electronically over networks by the command File ➤ Send Mail.

 **SEE ALSO** *Mail*

SMARTICONS

SmartIcons are graphic buttons, or *tools*, you click on with the mouse to trigger 1-2-3 commands or macros quickly, bypassing the menu system. Different sets, or *toolbars*, of SmartIcons are available for some menu commands and macros. You can also create new SmartIcons and assign them to custom macros.

SmartIcons that can be used to access other SmartIcon sets are shown in Figure II.20.

A listing of SmartIcons and their functions can be found on the inside front and back covers of this book.

To See an Explanation of an Icon

1. Move the pointer to the icon in the current toolbar and pause a moment.

or

Move the pointer to the icon, then click and hold the *right* mouse button.

2. An explanation will appear in a bubble beside the icon.

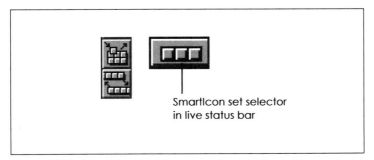

Smartlcon set selector
in live status bar

Figure II.20: SmartIcons and a button for working with SmartIcons

To Switch Toolbars

1. In the worksheet, select an object of the type to which the toolbar you want to change would apply: a range, a chart, a drawn object, or a query table. The default toolbar for the object type will appear: Default Sheet, Default Chart, Default Arrange, or Default Query.

2. To display a different toolbar, click the icon Select The Next Set Of Smartlcons. Another toolbar will appear. The display will cycle among the available toolbars *for the selected object type* each time you click the icon.

or

Click the Hide/Display Smartlcons button in the status bar. A pop-up menu listing the available named toolbars *for the selected object type* will appear. Click the name of the toolbar you want or select Hide Smartlcons from this menu to remove them from the screen.

To Rearrange the Icons in a Toolbar

1. Display the toolbar. (See "To Switch Toolbars" above.)

2. Press Ctrl as you drag any Smartlcon to a new position in the toolbar.

To Position Toolbars on the Screen

1. From the Tools pull-down menu, select Smartlcons. The Smartlcons dialog box will appear.

2. In the Position drop-down box, select the position on the screen at which toolbars will be displayed: Floating, Left, Top (the default), Right, or Bottom.

3. Select OK.

4. If you selected Floating in step 2, you can drag the toolbar to a desired position on the screen anytime during your work session.

To Customize Toolbars

1. In the worksheet, select an object of the type to which the toolbar you want to change would apply: a range, a chart, a drawn object, or a query table.

2. From the Tools pull-down menu, select SmartIcons. The SmartIcons dialog box will appear.

3. From the drop-down box at the top of this dialog box, select the name of the toolbar you wish to customize.

4. To add an icon to the named toolbar, drag it from the Available Icons list into the list of icons under the toolbar name drop-down box.

5. To delete an icon from the set, select it from the list under the toolbar name, then drag it outside the list.

6. To create spaces within a toolbar, drag the Spacer icon from the Available Icons list into the toolbar set to the location of the separation.

7. To rearrange icons in a set, drag an icon to its new position in the list.

8. To save the customized set as a new, named toolbar, select Save Set. The Save Set Of SmartIcons dialog box will appear. Type a new name in the Name Of Set text box, and select OK.

or

Select OK to save your customized set under the standard name shown above the icon list.

To Create New Icons

1. In the worksheet, select an object of the type to which the new icon would apply: a range, a chart, a drawn object, or a query table.

2. From the Tools pull-down menu, select SmartIcons. The SmartIcons dialog box will appear.

3. From the drop-down box, select the name of the set of icons to which the new one will be added.

4. Select Edit Icon. The Edit Icon dialog box will appear.

5. To modify an existing icon, select it from the Available Icons list, then choose Save As.

or

To create a new icon from scratch or to use an external bit-map as an icon, choose New Icon.

6. In the dialog box that appears, type a file name for the icon, and select OK.

7. Still in the Edit Icon dialog box, use the mouse to select colors from the palette beneath the enlarged icon button, and paint a new icon bitmap.

or

If you previously placed a bitmap on the Windows Clip-board, select the Paste Icon option.

8. Type the macro statements that the icon will execute in the Enter Macro Here box.

or

If you previously placed a macro on the Windows Clip-board, select Paste Macro.

9. Type the name of the command or action for the icon in the Description box.

10. Select OK to close the Edit Icon box, then OK to close the SmartIcons dialog box.

NOTES Don't confuse SmartIcons with *macro buttons,* which are a type of drawn object in 1-2-3. SmartIcons are displayed only in toolbars. A *macro button* is an embedded object in a worksheet file that can be located anywhere within a sheet. Like a custom Smart-Icon, a macro button can be used to trigger a sequence of macro commands.

The program desktop can display only one toolbar at a time. The toolbars that are available to you depend on the type of object currently selected in the worksheet. For example, you must select a chart to display the Default Chart toolbar.

If you select more than 26 icons for the current palette, specify Floating arrangement so that you can see them all.

Icon buttons are stored as bitmap files (.BMP), SmartIcon sets as .SMI files. These files are stored in different subdirectories, depending on the object type to which they apply: \SHEETICO (ranges), \DQAICO (query tables), \DRAWICO (drawn objects), \GRAPHICO (charts), \PREVICO (print ranges), and \TRANSICO (macro transcripts).

You can create your own icons with any graphics or paint program that generates bitmap files in .BMP format, including Windows Paintbrush, and follow the procedure described above to paste the image into a toolbar and define its macro.

 **SEE ALSO** *Buttons, Keyboard Shortcuts, Macros, Quick Menus*

SmartMasters are a set of templates (.WT4 files) provided with Release 5 that automate the creation of common types of business forms and reports.

To Create a Worksheet Using a SmartMaster

1. From the menu bar, select File ➤ New. (See *Notes* below.) The New File dialog box will appear.

2. Make a selection from the list of tasks. For example, choose Create An Invoice.

   or

   Select Browse to navigate the file system to select any .WT4 SmartMaster template file.

3. Select OK. The Table of Contents of the selected SmartMaster will appear.

4. Select the button in the Table of Contents *or* click the worksheet tab of the sheet you want to create. The sheet will open.

5. Type your data into the SmartMaster sheet: click a data-entry field, type your entry, and press ↵ or one of the arrow keys to move to the next field. (User entries are normally highlighted in blue; calculated values are shown in black.)

6. Select File ➤ Save.

7. Type a name for the new sheet.

8. Select OK.

NOTES The list of SmartMasters will not appear when you select File ➤ New if you have turned off the display of opening screens. To reset the program, select Tools ➤ User Setup and unmark the check box Skip New File And Welcome Screens.

Do not enter data into calculated fields (cells that contain formulas), unless you intend to modify the formula at that location.

OPTIONS The following buttons are available in most SmartMaster sheet displays:

Contents A worksheet tab representing the Table of Contents for the template.

Information Displays instructions on how to use the template.

Zoom Permits you to enlarge the view of the sheet.

Print Prints the sheet (an alternative to the File➤ Print command).

Sample Data　Fills in the template with typical data entries to illustrate what can be done with the template.

Keep Data　Saves the current set of data entries as a named scenario within the worksheet. (A worksheet can hold multiple scenarios.)

Swap Data　Toggles the display between sample data and your own data entries for purposes of comparison.

Tips　Displays instructions for specific parts of a form.

 SEE ALSO　*New File, Printing, Saving a File, User Setup*

SOLVER

The command Range ➤ Analyze ➤ Solver initiates Solver, a special feature of 1-2-3 that can solve for all variables in a complex worksheet model. Optionally, Solver can optimize one of the variables. Solver presents a range of possible answers, or combinations of variable values.

To Use Solver

1.　Set up a worksheet model designed for use with Solver. (See *Notes*, below, for requirements.)

2.　From the Range pull-down menu, select Analyze.

3.　From the Analyze cascade menu, select Solver.

4.　The Solver Definition dialog box appears. In the Adjustable Cells text box, enter cell addresses containing problem variables. Insert semicolons (;) as argument separators between multiple addresses.

5.　In the Constraint Cells text box, enter the range names or addresses that contain logical formulas for the answer.

6. Optionally, in the Optimal Cell text box, enter the range name or address of a cell to optimize. Select one of the option buttons, Max or Min, to maximize or minimize this cell's value in the solution.

7. Specify the number of values the Solver will find in the Number Of Answers text box.

8. Select Solve.

9. While the Solver is working, the Solver Progress dialog box appears with status information, including percent complete. To stop execution, select Cancel or press Ctrl-Break.

10. The Solver displays results in the Solver Answer dialog box. If no answers are found, you will be returned to step 4.

NOTES The three elements required of a model to be used with Solver are shown in the Solver Definition dialog box. Consider the elements as a set of problems in algebra. The Adjustable Cells are a set of variables. The Constraint Cells are a set of equations (logical formulas) containing the variables. The Optimal Cell, if you decide to use it, can be regarded as the ideal result, such as maximum return on investment or minimum cost.

OPTIONS If you specify an Optimal Cell in step 6, its contents must be variable, or it must contain a formula that refers to at least one variable cell. Selecting this option may reduce the number of answers that are required (or possible), both optimizing the solution and speeding execution. The number of answers (1–999) you specify in step 7 is approximate.

SEE ALSO *Backsolver, What-If Tables*

SORTING DATABASE RECORDS

The command Query ➤ Sort arranges records in the selected query
 table in the sort order you set. It works the same way as
Range ➤ Sort by permitting ascending or descending
order with primary and possibly also with secondary
sort keys.

SEE ALSO *Sorting a Range*

SORTING A RANGE

The command Range ➤ Sort rearranges data in a range in the order
you specify, such as alphabetic or numeric, ascending or descending.

Country
Sorting

New Feature The auxiliary application Country Sorting (usually installed in the Lotus Applications program group) has been provided to assist you in setting
up the proper sort order in 1-2-3 for different languages.

To Sort Data in a Range

1. In the current worksheet window, highlight a range (data
table) of records to be sorted.

2. From the Range pull-down menu, select Sort.

3. If you wish to override the range selected in step 1, specify a range name or address in the Range text box.

4. The All Keys text box shows multiple keys for further levels of sorting. Optionally, select the Add Keys button and enter the key, key range, and sort order in the Sort dialog box. Select Add Key for each level added, then select OK.

5. For each key, select Ascending or Descending for the order of the resulting list.

6. Optionally, to specify a subordinate order, enter a column address and sort order for a secondary key.

7. To enter new ranges in steps 3, 4, and 6, select Reset and repeat steps 3–6.

8. In the Sort dialog box, select OK.

NOTES   If the range you specify in step 1 is a database table, omit the first row containing the field names from the range address.

An example of a *primary key* would be a person's last name; the secondary key could be the first name. Extra keys might correspond to middle initials, zip codes, and so on.

OPTIONS   You can add multiple levels of keys in the of All Keys box in step 6. For each level, specify the number of the level in the Key text box and the database-table column of the sort key in the Key Range text box. Select Ascending or Descending order. Select Add Key to add the key to the list, and repeat the process until all numbered, subordinate sort keys have been defined. Then select OK.

 **SEE ALSO**   *Ranges, Sorting Database Records*

SPELLING

 The command Tools ➤ Spell Check checks text entries in worksheets or in selected ranges to correct your spelling.

To Spell Check

1. To check an area smaller than the current worksheet, select the range to be checked.

2. From the Tools pull-down menu, select Spell Check.

3. In the Check options box, select a option button to determine the extent of checking: Entire File (all sheets), Current Worksheet, or the selected Range.

4. If you selected Range in step 3 and you have not selected a range or wish to override your selection in step 1, type a range reference in the text box *or* click its button to use the Range Selector pointer to drag a range in the sheet.

5. If you wish, select the Options button to specify items to be included or ignored and select OK. (See *Options* below.)

6. Select OK.

7. If the program encounters a word not in its dictionary, it will highlight it as an Unknown Word in a dialog box. Retype the word in the Replace With box *or* click a suggestion from the listed words, and then Replace to change this instance of the word, Replace All to change all instances.

or

Select Skip to ignore this instance of the word, Skip All to ignore all instances.

or

Select Add To Dictionary to both skip all instances of the word and add it to the custom dictionary so it will be ignored in future checks.

8.   To terminate checking before the entire selection has been checked, select Close.

or

When the program notifies you that checking is complete, select OK.

 OPTIONS   For checking spelling include the following:

Check   Options determine the scope of the spelling check:

Entire File   Checks text entries in all worksheets, charts, query tables, and text blocks in the file. Select this option especially to check the spelling in chart titles, labels, and legends.

Current Worksheet   Checks text entries in all cells, query tables, and text blocks in the current worksheet.

Range   Checks text entries in all cells, query tables, and text blocks within the selected range.

Language Options   Selects a different language dictionary. The default is American (U.S. English).

Edit Dictionary   Permits you to add or delete words in the custom user dictionary file LTSUSER.DIC in the subdirectory LOTUS-APP\SPELL. (The LOTUSAPP directory and its dictionaries are shared by all Lotus Windows applications.)

Options (Button)   Check boxes, if marked, include the item and if unmarked, exclude the item, from the checking process:

Repeated Words   Checks for or ignores duplicate instances of the same word in the same place (*the the*).

Numbers   Checks for or ignores text that contains numeric digits (FILE1).

Initial Caps   Checks for or excludes words starting with capital letters, which might be proper names and therefore would not be in the dictionary.

Include User Dictionary Alternatives   If marked, accepts as correct words you have added to the custom dictionary.

Include Macro/@Function Keywords, Punctuation   Checks for or ignores the spelling and syntax of keyword commands and punctuation of arguments in macro statements and @functions.

 **SEE ALSO**   *User Setup*

SPLITTING A VIEW

The command View ➤ Split divides a worksheet window horizontally or vertically into two panes. Or, contiguous 3D worksheets can be displayed in perspective view. The split portions of windows are called *panes*. The purpose is to be able to view different parts of a large sheet at the same time. The View ➤ Clear Split command removes the effect.

To Divide a Worksheet into Window Panes

1.   Position the pointer in the row or column at which the split in the window will appear and click.

2.   From the View pull-down menu, select Split. The Split dialog box will appear.

3.   Under Type, select an option: Horizontal, Vertical, or Perspective. (See *Options*, below.)

4.   Optionally, mark the Synchronize Scrolling check box to cause views to scroll together, or in coordination.

5.   Select OK.

To Remove the Split from a Worksheet Window

•   From the View pull-down menu, select Clear Split.

NOTES To divide a window horizontally, move the mouse to the horizontal splitter at the top of the right scroll bar. When the pointer changes to a black two-headed vertical arrow, drag the pointer to the row where you want to divide the window.

To divide a window vertically, move the vertical splitter at the far left of the bottom scroll bar.

To move the pointer between panes, press F6 (Pane) in Ready or Point modes. Or, click the mouse on the cell you want.

If after you divide a worksheet document window, you reduce it to a size that causes the pointer to disappear, 1-2-3 automatically clears the split. To restore the split, increase the size of the worksheet window and repeat this procedure.

Any changes you might make in column widths, in hidden and displayed columns, and in worksheet titles on one pane are not reflected on other panes. When you clear a view with horizontal or vertical panes, 1-2-3 uses the settings from the top or left pane.

The program saves a file's window settings when you save the file.

OPTIONS Split options include Horizontal and Vertical panes. The Perspective option displays the same area of three contiguous worksheets in a 3D file and hides worksheet tabs. This is equivalent to arranging windows in *cascade* mode in Windows Program Manager.

In Perspective view, the following keys allow you to move the pointer:

F6 (Pane) Moves between worksheets in perspective view.

Ctrl-PageUp Moves the previous worksheet into view.

Ctrl-PageDown Moves the next worksheet into view.

Ctrl-Home Moves the pointer to the first cell in the first worksheet.

End-Ctrl-Home Moves the pointer to the last cell in the last worksheet.

SEE ALSO *Function Keys, Windows, Zooming*

SQL

SQL is an abbreviation for IBM's *structured query language,* by which databases can be manipulated. Lotus 1-2-3 for Windows permits you to link to external SQL databases and to issue commands in that language.

The 1-2-3 command Query ➤ Show SQL displays the SQL command equivalent for the current query.

To See the SQL Command for the Current Query

1. Select a query table. A bold border and handles should surround the table, and the Query selection should appear in the menu bar.

2. Perform any Query operation on the table.

3. From the Query pull-down menu, select Show SQL. The Show SQL dialog box will appear with the equivalent SQL command line displayed.

4. To copy the SQL statement to the Clipboard, select the Copy button, which also closes the dialog box.

or

Select Cancel to close the dialog box.

NOTES Copying the SQL command to the Clipboard allows you to paste it for later use with Tools ➤ Database ➤ Send Command or with the {send-sql} macro command.

 **SEE ALSO**   *Cutting Data to the Clipboard, External Databases, Pasting Data, Querying Databases*

STATUS BAR

The status bar appears across the bottom of the screen. Also called the *live status bar*, its buttons provide quick access to options such as number formats, fonts, point sizes, and SmartIcon sets. Messages also appear here about attributes of the current selection or status of the sheet. For example, if *CIRC* appears in a button, a circular reference exists in the sheet. Click the button, and the selection will move to the cell that holds the circular formula. Also, if *RECALC* appears, pressing that button will cause a required recalculation.

The elements of the live status bar and their functions are shown in Figure II.21.

 **SEE ALSO**   *Fonts and Attributes, SmartIcons, Styles*

STYLES

Styles are named sets of options for number and appearance formatting.

 **SEE ALSO**   *Gallery of Styles, Naming and Applying a Style, SmartMasters*

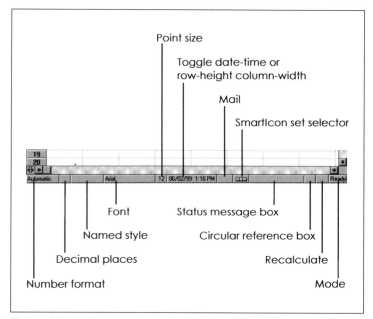

Figure II.21:   Elements of the live status bar

TABLES FOR EXTERNAL DATABASES

In some cases, the database driver you select with Tools ➤ Database ➤ Connect To External (DataLens) can create a table to hold the data that you extract. However, with some external database systems, you must use the Tools ➤ Database ➤ Create Table command to create the table in the process of connecting to the database. The command sets up a table definition that contains information on field names and widths, and data types. Optionally, you can use an existing table in 1-2-3 as a model, or you can modify the definition of an existing external table.

To Define a Table Using a Model in 1-2-3

1. Open the 1-2-3 file that contains the database table to be used as a model. (See *Notes*, below.)

  or

  Build a new database table in the current worksheet.

2. Select the model table.

3. From the Tools pull-down menu, select Database.

4. From the Database cascade menu, select Create Table.

5. In the Create Table dialog box, select the database driver and then select Continue.

6. Select the database name, then select Continue.

7. When the program prompts *Enter Table Name*, type a name for the new table.

8. Select Continue.

9. The program prompts *Model Table* and displays the reference to the range you selected in step 1. If you wish to override this selection, type a reference in the text box or click its button to use the Range Selector to drag a range in the sheet.

10. In the same dialog box, if required by the database driver, type a command, or *setup string,* in the syntax of the database language for creating the new table. (See *Options*, below.)

11. If you wish to insert the sample records from the model table into the new database table, mark the check box Insert Records From Model Table.

12. Select OK.

NOTES In 1-2-3, a *database table* is a range that contains one column for each field of a typical database record, ordered from left to right in the order the fields appear in the database records. The top row in the table contains column-heading labels that are used as field names. Column widths correspond to field lengths, and cell formatting controls data typing.

The 1-2-3 model is translated into a table definition in the database language, which, in turn, creates a new external table. The table definition that is passed to the database driver must have six columns, from left to right: Field Names, Data Types, Field Widths, Field Labels, Field Descriptions, and Field Creation Strings (see *Options*, below). SQL and dBASE IV drivers use only columns 1–3 and 6. Paradox uses only columns 1–3. In any case, columns 4 and 5 must be present.

Requirements for database connection, table setup command strings, and table structure vary, depending on the system being accessed.

 **OPTIONS** Paradox users must supply one of the following setup strings in step 10 to determine the sort order for the table: SORT ASCII, SORT INTL (international ASCII), SORT NORDAN (Norwegian and Danish), or SORT SWEDFIN (Swedish and Finnish). (The sort order in 1-2-3 can be set up by using the Country Sorting application.)

 SEE ALSO *External Databases, Querying Databases, Sorting Database Records*

TEMPLATES

Templates are predefined worksheets containing layout, formulas, and formatting, but empty of data, that can be used as guides for preparing similar sheets. In 1-2-3, templates are stored as .WT4 files.

 SEE ALSO *Gallery of Styles, Saving a File, SmartMasters*

TRANSCRIPTS OF MACROS

Transcripts of macros are listings of macro command equivalents for the actions and selections you perform when recording a macro (initiated by the command Tools ➤ Macro ➤ Record).

The command Tools ➤ Macro ➤ Show Transcript displays and Tools ➤ Macro ➤ Hide Transcript hides a document window that contains the macro command listing (see *Macros* for procedures).

The command Transcript ➤ Minimize On Run shrinks this window to an icon whenever you play back a macro with the command Transcript ➤ Playback. The recording of cell addresses as relative offsets or as absolute references can be controlled by the commands Transcript ➤ Record Relative and Transcript ➤ Record Absolute. (The Transcript pull-down menu item will appear on the menu bar only when the Transcript document window is open.)

TRANSCRIPT ➤ MINIMIZE ON RUN

This command reduces the Transcript window to an icon and makes it inactive when you play back the macro with Tools ➤ Macro ➤ Run or Transcript ➤ Playback, permitting you to view the entire 1-2-3 desktop during macro execution.

To Minimize the Transcript Window When Running a Macro

1. Make the Transcript window active by clicking its title bar *or* pressing Ctrl-F6. The Transcript selection will appear in the menu bar.

2. From the Transcript pull-down menu, select Minimize On Run.

3. Start the macro with Tools ➤ Macro ➤ Run *or* Transcript ➤ Playback *or* an equivalent action. The Transcript window will shrink to an icon and the macro will play back.

NOTES   This command is a toggle, which can be on or off. After you choose this command the first time to turn the feature on, a check mark appears next to the Minimize On Run item in the menu. The Transcript window retains the current setting for this command until you turn it off or exit 1-2-3.

To restore the Transcript window to its original size, click the control box of an open Transcript window and choose Restore or double-click the minimized Transcript window icon.

If you do not use Minimize On Run, the Transcript window becomes inactive on macro playback, but it is not reduced to an icon.

TRANSCRIPT ➤ PLAYBACK

The command Transcript ➤ Playback starts the Macro Translator and plays back commands from the Transcript window as a macro. The purpose of this command is to play back the contents of the Transcript window before the sequence has been saved as a named macro or assigned to a button.

Before starting macro playback, make sure that your current selection in the worksheet is the cell or range that you want the macro commands to affect.

To Play Back a Macro

1.   Select the keystrokes in the Transcript window to play back.

2.   From the Transcript pull-down menu, select Playback.

TRANSCRIPT ➤ RECORD ABSOLUTE OR TRANSCRIPT ➤ RECORD RELATIVE

This pair of toggle commands causes cell addresses appearing in the open Transcript window to be recorded either as absolute (fixed) references (using explicit cell addresses) or as relative (using offsets from the current cell) references.

When the current setting is Record Absolute, the command Record Relative appears in the Transcript pull-down menu, and vice versa. Set the command as needed just prior to selecting Tools ➤ Macro ➤ Record.

 **SEE ALSO** *Buttons, Macros, Ranges*

TRANSPOSING A RANGE

The command Range ➤ Transpose copies data from one range to another. In the process, the arrangement of the data is transposed (horizontal to vertical or vertical to horizontal), and all formulas are converted to values.

To Copy and Transpose Data

1. Be sure all formula calculations and data links are updated.

2. In the current worksheet window, highlight a range of data to be transposed.

3. From the Range pull-down menu, select Transpose.

4. The Range Transpose dialog box appears. If you wish to override the range selected in step 1, specify a range name or address in the From text box.

5. Enter the destination range in the To text box. (The address of the first cell is sufficient.)

6. Select OK.

7. If you specified three-dimensional ranges, the Transpose Options dialog box appears. Select options (see *Options* below) and then select OK.

NOTES Transposing data causes columns to be converted to rows, and vice versa. Addresses are adjusted accordingly.

If you specify a three-dimensional range in the From text box, there should be at least the same number of sheets in the To range.

OPTIONS For three-dimensional transpositions, selections in the dialog box in step 7 are the following:

Rows/Columns Transposes rows (horizontally arranged data) so they become columns within each worksheet.

Columns/Worksheets Copies each column in the From range in sequence to become a row in a different worksheet in the To range.

Worksheets/Rows Copies each row from each worksheet in the From range in sequence to become a column in a different worksheet in the To range.

SEE ALSO *Copying Data to the Clipboard, Pasting Data*

UNDO

When the selection Undo is not dimmed in the Edit pull-down menu, selecting it will cancel the result of the most recent reversible command.

To Undo a Command

- *Before you execute another command*, select Undo from the Edit pull-down menu.

  or

  Press Ctrl-Z or Alt-Backspace.

NOTES If Undo is dimmed in the Edit pull-down menu, there is nothing in the command buffer (nothing to undo). After you select Edit ➤ Undo, the command is dimmed and cannot be reversed (you can't undo Edit ➤ Undo itself). You will not be able to select Edit ➤ Undo if there is no more available memory.

Certain functions cannot be reversed, including F5 (Go To), F6 (Pane), and F9 (Calc). You also cannot undo effects of Print commands, File commands, or pointer movements.

SEE ALSO *Clearing Data from cells*

UPDATING A DATABASE QUERY

The command Query ➤ Refresh Now updates the currently selected query table, and optionally the source database as well. The command Query ➤ Update Database Table transfers the results of a query to the original database table from which the query table was extracted.

QUERY ➤ REFRESH NOW

 This command updates records in a query table, potentially also making changes to database tables, query options, criteria, aggregates, or field names.

To Update Query Results

1. Select a query table. A bold border and handles should surround the table, and the Query selection should appear in the menu bar.

2.   From the Query pull-down menu, select Refresh Now.

or

Press F7 (Query).

NOTES   To automatically update the query table when you make changes to its entries, select Query ➤ Set Options ➤ Auto Refresh.

Once you have selected Refresh Now, processing starts and you cannot interrupt the query. If you are unsure of the fields in a long query, remember to limit the number of records returned to shorten the query. Before you do this command, select Query ➤ Set Criteria and mark the Set Limit check box. Specify a small number of records, and select OK.

QUERY ➤ UPDATE DATABASE TABLE

This command applies changes in query table records to the original database table from which the query table was extracted.

To Update a Database Table

1.   Select a query table that you want to change. A bold border and handles should surround the table, and the Query selection should appear in the menu bar.

2.   Edit the records of the table by changing cell contents directly or by performing Query operations.

3.   From the Query pull-down menu, select Update Database Table. (See *Notes* below.) Changes in query table records are updated in the database.

NOTES   This command not only changes the values in the original database, but also updates the sort order of all the records that appear in the query, and only those records.

In step 3 of "To Update a Database Table," the option Update Database Table will be dimmed unless you mark the Allow Updates To Database Table check box in Query ➤ Set Options. Once the table has been updated, the option will be dimmed again.

 **SEE ALSO** *Criteria for Queries, Joining Database Queries, Querying Databases*

USER SETUP

The command Tools ➤ User Setup permits you to set various 1-2-3 program parameters, including default worksheet directory, user options, clock display, international formats, and recalculation options.

To Set User Options

1. From the Tools pull-down menu, select User Setup.

2. The User Setup dialog box appears. Select any of the check boxes to set user options: Drag And Drop Cells, Use Automatic Format, Save Every *(N)* Minutes, Undo, Run Autoexecute Macros, Beep On Error, and Number Of Recent Files To Show *(M)*.

3. To set international display formats, select the International button. The International dialog box appears. Make settings and then select OK. (See *Options*, below.)

4. To set recalculation options, select the Recalculation button. The Recalculation dialog box appears. Make settings and then select OK. (See *Options*, below.)

5. If you wish, retype your name in the Name text box.

6. To change the default worksheet directory, enter a device and path in the Worksheet Directory text box.

7. Select OK.

NOTES These options are saved in the file 123R5.INI and will affect this and future work sessions until you change the settings. An exception is Recalculation options, which are saved with the worksheet file.

Options you choose using Tools ➤ User Setup ➤ International override those you set in Windows Control Panel International, but only for use with 1-2-3.

The default sort order in 1-2-3 can be set by using the Country Sorting application, which is installed automatically in the Lotus Applications program group when you set up 1-2-3. To access Country Sorting, exit 1-2-3, open or switch to the Lotus Applications group, and double-click the Country Sorting icon.

Options (Check Boxes) If these check boxes are marked, they permit the following options; if they are unmarked, they disable the following options:

Skip New File And Welcome Screens Turns off display of the first two dialog boxes when you start a program session, and also supresses the New File dialog box when you select File ➤ New. Turn off the option if you mostly want to start with blank worksheets rather than templates.

Drag-And-Drop Cells Enables the ability to copy cell contents by dragging with the mouse while the Ctrl key is pressed and to move cell contents by dragging. These are shortcut alternatives to Edit ➤ Copy or Edit ➤ Cut and Edit ➤ Paste.

Confirm Drag-And-Drop Displays a prompt requesting confirmation before overwriting data at the new location.

Use Automatic Format If marked, uses Automatic as the default number format setting. If unmarked, the default is General.

Save Every *(N)* Minutes Causes the program to automatically back up your worksheets to disk every $N = 1$–99 minutes.

Undo Turns on the ability to reverse the previous command or action. (Unmarking this option can save memory.)

Run Autoexecute Macros Executes the macro automatically when a file containing it is opened.

Beep On Error   Sounds the computer bell on program errors and on the macro command {beep}.

Refresh File Links Automatically   Automatically updates data links between linked documents. Otherwise, a program prompt appears each time a link must be updated.

Number Of Recent Files To Show   Shows you the $M = 0$–5 most recently opened file names when you activate File pull-down menu. You can then select File ➤ <filename> instead of selecting File ➤ Open and possibly having to navigate the file system.

Name   Shows the user's name as entered during installation.

Worksheet Directory   Shows the default path for storage of worksheet files.

International   These options affect formatting of dates and times, translation of characters, use of symbols and separators, and display of monetary values:

Format   Select Date and Time display formats from the examples in the drop boxes. These settings apply only to Short International options.

File Translation   Specify whether .WK1 worksheets and other foreign character-data files will be translated according to the Lotus International Character Set (LICS) or ASCII in the 1-2-3 Rel 2 (DOS) drop-down box. In the Text File drop-down box, specify whether imported or created text files will be translated in International format or according to the current system Country setting (IBM Code Page in DOS).

Style   For punctuation and argument separators, select among eight numbered styles in the drop-down box. For display of negative values, select between Parentheses (numbers enclosed in parentheses) and Sign (leading minus) in the drop-down box. (Remember that display of either of these alternatives in red is a further global option in Style ➤ Worksheet Defaults.)

Currency   For the Default currency format, select any one of 43 predefined formats. Or, select Other Country for a user-defined format. (See *Currency Formatting*.) In the Display Currencies Using box, select Symbols for currency signs or ISO for text abbreviations specified by the International Standards Organization.

Recalculation   Options here affect the updating of formulas and the handling of circular references:

Recalculation   Select either Automatic (immediately after each new entry) or Manual (only when you press F9 (Calc)). Select Manual to improve performance with large or complex sheets.

Order of Recalculation   Select one: Natural (recalculate source formulas first), By Column (left to right by column, from the top to the bottom sheet), or By Row (top to bottom by row, from the top to the bottom sheet).

Iterations   Enter a number (1–50) for the number of column-wise or rowwise passes to limit recalculation. Or, specify a limit when you have selected Natural and the program attempts to resolve circular references (recursions).

👁 **SEE ALSO**   *Currency Formatting, Number Formatting, Sorting a Range, Worksheet Defaults*

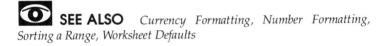

VERSION MANAGER

The command Range ➤ Version activates the Version Manager, which can be used to create different sets of data (*versions*) for the same range, permitting you to try different sets of assumptions for what-if analysis. You can create, update, and delete versions and change information saved with a version. A group of versions can be saved in a *scenario* (for example, best- and worst-case scenarios). Different versions can be managed with the Version Manager Index.

To Name a Range and Create a Version of the Range

1. Enter the data for the version in the worksheet.

2. Select the range that holds the data you entered in step 1.

3. From the Range pull-down menu, select Version.

4. The Version Manager dialog box appears.

5. Select the Create button.

6. The Create Version dialog box appears. In the Named range, specify a range to hold the version.

7. In the Version name box, type the name of the new version.

8. Optionally, in the Comment text box, enter a comment about the version.

9. To save style information with the version, mark the Retain Styles check box.

10. Select a sharing option: Unprotected, Protected, or Protected & Hidden.

11. Select OK.

To Display a Version in the Worksheet

1. From the Range pull-down menu, select Version.

2. The Version Manager dialog box appears. In the Named Range drop-down box, select the range for which you want to show a version.

3. In the With Version(s) drop-down box, select which version to show in the worksheet.

4. Select OK.

To Add Version Comments
in the Version Manager

1.   From the Range pull-down menu, select Version.

2.   In the Version Manager, select the Info button, and the Version Info dialog box appears. In the Comment text box, type a comment.

3.   Select OK.

4.   To see a comment in the Version Manager, resize the Version Manager dialog box vertically by dragging its borders until the comment appears.

NOTES   You can create versions of named ranges only. You can name the range in the Create Version dialog box, or you can use Range ➤ Name ➤ Add to name the range before creating the version.

Only named ranges containing 2,000 or fewer cells are permitted with multiple versions.

Use the Version Manager to work with one version of a range. Switch to the Version Manager Index to change versions or scenarios.

Displaying different versions in the worksheet can overwrite the same range. So to avoid losing your data, in the Version Manager use Create Version (Alt-C) or Update Version (Alt-U).

OPTIONS   Different sets of controls and options are available in the Version Manager and in the Version Manager Index. In either dialog box, the two buttons in the bottom right corner toggle the modes Highlight (marking ranges with versions) and Tracking (navigating among ranges with versions). (Keyboard shortcuts: Alt-H and Alt-K.)

Version Manager Options   When you create a range, the Version Manager places a check mark next to its name in the With Version(s) drop-down box. When you update this range, Version

Manager places a line through the check mark and changes the font to italics in the With Version(s) drop-down box.

Create Creates a new version by your selecting Range and Version names, adding Comments, specifying a Sharing option, and possibly retaining Styles. Sharing options are Unprotected (the default), Protected, and Protected & Hidden. (Keyboard shortcut: Alt-C.)

Update Updates a version with data and styles. (Keyboard shortcut: Alt-U.)

Info Opens a Version Info dialog box, which allows you to create comments, to show a person's name and date of changes in the Modified By text box, to select Sharing options, and to retain styles. (Keyboard shortcut: Alt-I.)

Delete Deletes a saved version or scenario. (Keyboard shortcut: Alt-D.)

Close Closes the Version Manager. (Keyboard shortcut: Alt-L.)

To Index Opens the Version Manager Index dialog box for listing and accessing several versions of a range. (Keyboard Shortcut: Alt-T.)

Version Manager Index
The Version Manager Index has the following options:

Collapse/Expand (Upper-left button) Lets you see or hide the details associated with Version and Scenario names. (Keyboard shortcut: Alt-+ on numeric keypad.)

Date Sort Sorts the index by names of Ranges, Versions, Scenarios, Date, or Contributors. (Keyboard shortcut: Alt-O.)

Current Version Shown Selects for viewing All, Current, New Only, Protected Only, Hidden Only, or Unsaved versions. (Keyboard shortcut: Alt-N.)

Clipboard button Copies the index to the Clipboard. (Keyboard shortcut: Alt-A.)

Comment button Displays or hides comments for the selected version. (Keyboard shortcut: Alt-E.)

Shared File Updates a version that has been already saved using File ➤ Protect.

Read Status Marks all unread versions as read.

Clipboard   Copies version information to the Windows Clipboard.

Comments   Shows or hides the comment field.

Create   Same as in Version Manager.

Scenario   Groups versions into a scenario, adds a Scenario Name, adds Comments, selects Sharing options, and adds from the list of Available Versions to a group of Selected Versions. (Keyboard shortcut: Alt-S.)

Update   Same as in Version Manager.

Info   Same as in Version Manager.

Delete   Same as in Version Manager.

Show   Opens a previously created version or scenario. (Keyboard shortcut: Alt-W.)

Report   Creates version reports (starting with REPORT01.WK4) showing selected outcomes of a formula. You can Include Version Data or Audit Information, arranging data either by Columns or by Rows. (Keyboard shortcut: Alt-P.)

Merge   Opens and merges previously created versions or scenarios from one file to another. (Keyboard shortcut: Alt-M.)

Close   Closes the Version Manager. (Keyboard shortcut: Alt-L.)

To Manager   Closes the Version Manager Index and opens the Version Manager dialog box. (Keyboard shortcut: Alt-T.)

 **SEE ALSO**   *Naming a Range, Protecting Ranges and Files, What-If Tables*

VIEWING PREFERENCES

The command View ➤ Set View Preferences establishes your predefined settings for viewing the worksheet for the current file and for future sessions of 1-2-3.

To Set Viewing Preferences

1. From the View pull-down menu, select Set View Preferences.

2. In the Show In Current File box, mark the check boxes of options you wish to enable. (See *Options*, below.)

3. To change the Worksheet Frame, select a frame type from the drop-down box.

4. To change the color of Grid Lines, select a color from the drop-down color palette.

5. To change the default display size of cells, specify a new size in Custom Zoom %.

6. Under Show In 1-2-3, select the check box of any of the following options: SmartIcons, Edit Line, and Status Bar.

7. Select OK.

NOTES The Options under Show In 1-2-3 become the default settings for all worksheets in memory and for new worksheets in this and future sessions.

OPTIONS In the dialog box in steps 2–6 the options are as follows:

Show In Current File Choose from these options:

Worksheet Frame Displays the row and column borders in Standard (lettered columns and numbered rows), Characters (shows character count for widths of columns and heights of rows), or numeric rulers marked off in Inches, Metric, or Points/Picas.

Worksheet Tabs If marked, displays folder tabs at the top of worksheet windows for naming and accessing sheets in 3D files.

Grid Lines Choose a color for grid lines in the sheet from the palette in this drop-down box. You can also omit the grid altogether by selecting a transparent color or by clearing the Grid Lines check box.

Scroll Bars   If marked, shows (or if unmarked, hides) the scroll bars at the bottom and right margins.

Page Breaks   If marked, shows (or if unmarked, hides) the appearance of page breaks as dotted lines in the worksheet.

Charts, Drawings, and Pictures   If marked, shows (or if unmarked, hides) the graphic elements charts, drawings, and pictures in the worksheet. If you place a chart or drawing in the worksheet, then unmark this check box, the chart or drawing will still be there—it will just not be displayed.

Custom Zoom <number>%   Changes the display size of cells from full screen, or 100%, to sizes 25–400%.

Make Default   Updates global preferences for future sessions. Otherwise, only the current session is affected.

Show In 1-2-3   Choose from these options:

SmartIcons   If marked, shows (or if unmarked, hides) the SmartIcon toolbars.

Edit Line   If marked, shows (or if unmarked, hides) the Edit Line at the top of the screen in which the contents of a selected cell may be displayed and edited.

Status Bar   If marked, shows (or if unmarked, hides) the status bar at the bottom of the screen.

 **SEE ALSO**   *Charting, Drawing, Page Break, SmartIcons, Zooming*

WHAT-IF TABLES

The command Range ➤ Analyze ➤ What-If Table substitutes values for 1–3 variables in a formula (called a *1-,2-, or 3-way analysis*). Two types of analysis can be performed: *sensitivity analysis* or *cross-tabulation*. In sensitivity analysis, variables in formulas are simply substituted and the results output to a range. In cross-tabulation, a database @function is applied to a database table. The purpose of what-if analysis is to test the results of different assumptions on a formula or a set of formulas.

SmartIcons for creating and cross-tabulating a what-if table are shown in Figure II.22.

To Perform Sensitivity Analysis

1. Identify a *table range* in the current worksheet to hold the table that will be generated. (If you specify a 3-way analysis, compose the table of multiple, contiguous sheets.)

2. Select a location outside the range for 1–3 input cells. Label the cells so that you can refer to them in later steps. Leave the contents of the cell(s) blank. (One cell is required for each dimension of the analysis: 1 cell for 1-way, 2 cells for 2-way, 3 cells for 3-way.)

3. In the worksheet, enter the formula(s) to be analyzed. (See *Notes*, below, for specific locations for each type of analysis.)

4. Enter values into the table range. (See *Notes*, below, for requirements.)

5. From the Range menu, select Analyze.

6. From the Analyze cascade menu, select What-If Table.

7. From the What-If Table dialog box, select in the Number of variables pull-down either a 1-,2-, or 3-Way analysis. (See *Options*, below.)

8. From the What-If Table dialog box, enter the range you set up in step 1 in the Table Range box.

Figure II.22: SmartIcons for creating and cross-tabulating a what-if table

9. For 3-Way Analysis only, enter the cell address that holds the formula to analyze in the Formula Cell text box.

10. Enter the cell addresses of the input cells in text box Input Cell 1–3.

11. Select OK.

To Perform Cross-Tabulation

1. Identify a *database table* (special type of 1-2-3 range) that holds the records to be analyzed.

2. Set up a table range in the current worksheet. For 3-way analysis, you will need multiple sheets, one for each value to be input to the third variable.

3. Set up a *criteria range*. (See *Notes*.)

4. Select a cell outside the table range and enter a database @function to be applied to the table.

5. Perform steps 3–11 of *To Perform Sensitivity Analysis* above.

To Reset Ranges

1. Select the file document window that contains the what-if table to be reset.

2. From the Range pull-down menu, select Analyze.

3. From the Analyze cascade menu, select What-If Table.

4. From the What-If Table dialog box, select Reset.

5. All input cell, formula, and table ranges in the what-if tables in the file will be cleared.

NOTES In 1-2-3, a *database table* is a range that contains one column for each field of a typical database record. The requirements for setting up table ranges for sensitivity analysis and cross-tabulation differ. Requirements also vary by the number of dimensions involved in the analysis.

Sensitivity Analysis Input cell addresses or their labels
should be used as variable names in your formulas. You never enter
data directly into the input cells. The program uses them as *buffers*,
or working memory areas, and each input cell must be referenced
in each formula to be tested. You enter data values in the table range;
the program places the results of the analysis there, as well. The table
range must be set up in steps 2 and 3 as follows:

1-Way Analysis Leave the cell in the upper-left corner of the
table range blank. Enter the formula(s) to be analyzed in the remaining cells in the first row. Enter the data values that will be
substituted in the formula in the first column, starting at the
second cell (upper-left cell blank).

2-Way Analysis Enter a single formula in the upper-left cell
of the table range. The formula must refer to both of the input
cells you set up in step 2. In the first column (starting with the
second cell, beneath the formula), enter the data values to be
substituted for input cell 1. In the row to the right of the formula, enter the data values to be substituted for input cell 2.
Results for each pair of variables will be displayed at the intersection of the corresponding column and row in the table.

3-Way Analysis Compose the table range of multiple sheets
(a three-dimensional range). You will need a sheet for each
data value you enter for the third input cell, or variable. Enter
a single formula at a location *outside* the table range. The formula must refer to each of the three input cells you set up in
step 2. When you begin to build the table range, leave the upper-left cell in all sheets blank. In the first column of the first
sheet (starting with the second cell), enter data values for input
cell 1. Use Edit ➤ Copy to copy this column of data to all the
other sheets in the table range. In the first row of the first sheet,
enter data values for input cell 2. Copy this row to all sheets.
Finally, enter data values for input cell 3 in the upper-left cell
of each sheet. Results are shown in the cell at the three-
dimensional intersection of the three variables.

Cross-Tabulation In cross-tabulation, each database @function
must use the database table as its input range, a field name ("*fieldname*")
for data values, and the criteria range. (The input range can be an external table.) You specify labels or values from the database as data

values in the table range. (You never make entries directly into the input cells. The program uses them as buffers.) Results are displayed in the table range. To begin building the criteria range and table range, in step 3 create a two-row criteria range that does not lie within the table range. Further steps are as follows:

1-Way Analysis   Copy one field name (the selection criterion) from the database table to one of the blank rows. The cell just below it will be the input cell (enter this address in step 10). In the table range, leave the cell in the upper-left corner blank. Enter one or more database @functions in the remaining cells in the first row. Enter the data values to be used in the tabulation in the first column, starting at the second cell (upper-left cell blank).

2-Way Analysis   Copy two field names (the selection criteria) from the database table to one of the blank rows. The cell just below each field name will be the input cells 1 and 2 (enter these addresses in step 10). In the table range, enter a single database @function in the top-left cell. In the first column (starting at the second cell, beneath the formula), enter the data value for cell 1. In the row to the right of the formula, enter the data values for input cell 2. Results for each pair of variables will be displayed at the intersection of the corresponding column and row in the table range.

3-Way Analysis   Copy three field names (the selection criteria) from the database table to one of the blank rows. The cell just below each field name will be the input cells 1, 2, and 3 (enter these addresses in step 10). Compose the table range of multiple sheets (a three-dimensional range). You will need a sheet for each data value you enter for the third input cell, or variable. Enter a single database @function at a location *outside* the criteria and table ranges. When you begin to build the table range, leave the upper-left cell blank. In the first column (starting at the second cell), enter the data value for input cell 1. Use Edit ► Copy to copy this column of data to all other sheets in the table range. In the first row of the first sheet, enter data values for input cell 2. Copy this to all sheets. Finally, enter the data values for input cell 3 in the upper-left cell of each sheet. Results are shown in the cell at the three dimensional intersection of the three variables.

SEE ALSO *Aggregating Database Queries, Backsolver, Cross-Tabulation, External Databases, Querying Databases, Solver*

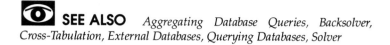

WINDOWS

There are two types of windows: *application windows* in which programs run and *document windows* in which file contents are displayed. Here are summarized ways of manipulating windows in Windows and in 1-2-3.

THE CONTROL MENU

The small bar in the box in the upper-left corner of the current window is the access point to the control menu for that window.

To Control an Open Window

1. Click on the window's control box.

or

If the window is the 1-2-3 application window itself or any dialog box, press Alt-spacebar. For any other window within 1-2-3, press Alt--.

2. The control menu appears. Make a selection by clicking on the item, pressing its underscored letter, or pressing the accelerator key listed to the right of the item.

or

If you selected with one of the Alt speed keys, you can use the arrows keys to move the highlight and press ↵ to choose.

NOTES   In 1-2-3, worksheets are displayed in document windows. Since the number of worksheet files that can be open concurrently is limited only by the amount of available memory, multiple document windows may be open on the desktop (screen) at the same time. Use the Next command in the control menu to move from one worksheet to another.

OPTIONS   Options in the control menu that drops down from the upper-left corner of any window include the following (dimmed commands cannot be chosen):

Restore   After a window has been maximized (enlarged) or minimized (shrunk), restores it to its former size.

Move   Lets you move the window to another location on the desktop (screen) by using the arrow keys or dragging the title bar to a new location with the mouse.

Size   Lets you change the size of a window by using the arrow keys or by dragging an edge or corner to a new location with the mouse. Dialog boxes cannot be resized.

Minimize   Shrinks the window to an icon.

Maximize   Enlarges the window to the largest size that can be displayed on the screen.

Close   Terminates the running of the window's task or closes the file it represents. The accelerator key for this command is Ctrl-F4.

Next   When multiple document windows are displayed, switches to the next open document. The accelerator key for this command is Ctrl-F6.

Paste   In Windows 3.1, you can copy text from the *Clipboard*, or scratch-pad memory area of Windows, into a document window of a non-Windows application. (In Windows applications, you would typically do Edit ➤ Paste instead.)

Edit, Settings, Fonts   Appear only on Windows control menus. These apply to non-Windows (DOS) applications in 386 Enhanced mode and are not available with 1-2-3. The Edit command displays a cascading menu of Clipboard operations, Settings controls display and multitasking, and Fonts allows you to alter the way text is displayed in the window. Use them when running other applications, such as database programs, concurrently with 1-2-3 for Windows.

Switch To   Lets you change to a different application by using the Windows Task List (a listing of currently running programs). The accelerator key for this command is Ctrl-Esc.

MINIMIZE/MAXIMIZE

In Windows and in 1-2-3, application (task) or document (work-sheet) windows can be minimized (shrunk to an icon) or maximized (enlarged to fill the desktop). Minimize a window to keep it ready while making room on the desktop for other windows or to reduce its processing priority or memory allocation. Maximize a window to have more room to work within it or to give it higher processing priority and more memory.

The Restore button returns a maximized window to its normal size:

To Minimize or Maximize a Window

1.   Click on either the Minimize (▼) or Maximize (▲) buttons in the top right corner of the window's title bar and omit step 2.

or

Press Alt-- to activate the window's control menu.

2.   From the control menu, select Minimize or Maximize.

To Restore a Window to Its Previous Size

1. If the window has been shrunk to an icon, double-click on the icon. If the window has been maximized, click on the Restore button in the top-right corner of its menu bar and omit step 2.

or

Press Alt-- to activate the window's control-menu box.

2. From the control Pull-Down menu, select Restore.

NOTES In step 1, if the window is the 1-2-3 application window itself or any dialog box, the keyboard command for accessing its Control menu is Alt-spacebar.

NOTES ON MANIPULATING WINDOWS

Any application (task) window or document (worksheet) window in 1-2-3 can be moved or adjusted in size on the desktop (screen).

To Move a Window

1. Drag the title bar of the window to the new position and omit steps 2–4.

or

Press Alt-- to activate the window's control menu.

2. From the control menu, select Move.

3. Use the arrow keys (← ↑ ↓ →) to move the window to the new position.

4. Press ↵.

To Resize a Window

1. Drag one of the borders or corners of the window to a new position and skip steps 2–4.

or

Press Alt-- to activate the window's control menu.

2. From the control menu, select Size.

3. Use the arrow keys (← ↑ ↓ →) to move the window's borders to new positions.

4. Press ↵.

NOTES Dialog boxes cannot be resized, but can be moved by dragging the title bar. To gain control of the application window or a dialog box when using the keyboard in step 1, press Alt-spacebar instead.

MANIPULATING WORKSHEET WINDOWS IN 1-2-3

Commands in the Window pull-down menu can be used to arrange document windows on the 1-2-3 desktop.

To Arrange Document Windows

1. To view windows stacked on top of one another, from the menu bar, select Window ➤ Cascade.

or

To view windows side-by-side, select Window ➤ Tile.

2. Manipulate the positions and sizes of the windows to adjust the view. (See *Notes on Manipulating Windows* above.)

To Switch between Open Document Windows

• From the menu bar, select Window <title>.

or

• If the window is visible, click anywhere inside it.

NOTES You can have several document windows open in 1-2-3 at the same time. The titles of all open windows will appear in the Window pull-down menu. The active window will be marked with a ✓.

 **SEE ALSO** *Viewing   Preferences,   Worksheet   Defaults, Zooming*

WORKSHEET DEFAULTS

The command Style ➤ Worksheet Defaults sets various parameters that affect the display of the current worksheet and its value formats. These settings are *global*, or affect all default settings and formats in the entire sheet, and may be overridden by explicit commands such as Style ➤ Alignment and Style ➤ Column Width. Settings apply to all sheets in the current file if Group mode is turned on in this command's options.

To Make Global Worksheet Settings

1. Move the pointer into the worksheet document window to be affected and click to activate the window.

2. From the Style pull-down menu, select Worksheet Defaults.

3. In the Worksheet Defaults dialog box, you can reset the following options: Font (type Face and Size), Numbers Format, Colors, and Other. (See *Options* below.)

4. In the Numbers Format text box, select the Format drop-down box to change the display formats of numbers, labels, dates, and times.

5. Also in the Numbers Format text box, select options for Decimal Places and Parentheses.

6. Select OK.

NOTES If you specify anything other than General in Format options, the Decimal Places text box will appear, in which you must enter the number of digits to appear to the right of the decimal point.

OPTIONS   Options in the dialog box in step 3 include the following:

Font   Select the default type Face and Size for text and data from the list of installed TrueType and ATM fonts. (See *Fonts and Attributes*.)

Optionally, select the Make Default button to apply this font to future work sessions.

Number Format   Options here control the display of values and text in worksheet cells:

> **Format**   Select among: Automatic (defaults for all types of values), Fixed (truncated to your specified number of Decimal places from 1–15), Scientific (powers of 10), Currency (sign and decimal), Comma (thousands separator), General (the default for numbers, no thousands separator), +/− (bar-graph equivalent), Percent (calculated, with % sign), Text (formulas as text, numbers as General), Hidden (not printed), Automatic (program determines best fit), Label (label prefix (') added automatically), or various date and time formats. (See *Number Formatting*.)

> **Display Zeros As**   If the contents of a cell equal zero, shows the results as zeros, leaves zeros blank, or uses a label (enter a label in the text box).

> **Parentheses**   If marked, encloses *all* default formated values in parentheses (), not just negative values.

Other   These options affect the layout of the current sheet or, optionally, all sheets in the current file:

> **Column Width**   Can be a value from 1–240 for the global width of all columns in the worksheet. Individual columns can be adjusted with the Style ➤ Column Width command.

> **Alignment**   Controls the positioning of text labels, or alphanumeric data preceded by a label prefix. Select Left, Center, or Right to justify the string in the column.

> **Group Mode**   If marked, turns mode on and off. When on, settings in this dialog box will affect all sheets in the current file.

Colors These options affect the appearance of displays on the computer screen. (In monochrome printouts, color settings will be translated to grayscale values by the Windows printer driver.)

Text Can be any color from a palette of 256 that appears when you select the drop-down button.

Cell Background Can be any solid color from a palette of 256 that appears when you select the drop-down button.

Worksheet Tab Can be any solid color from a palette of 256 that appears when you select the drop-down button.

Negative Values In Red If marked, displays negative numeric values in red.

Display Windows Defaults If marked, uses the color palette as defined in Windows Control Panel ➤ Colors.

 SEE ALSO *Column Width, Currency Formatting, Fonts and Attributes, Lines and Object Colors, Number Formatting*

ZOOMING

Reducing or enlarging the view of the worksheet in the 1-2-3 document window can be performed by the commands View ➤ Custom <percentage>%, View ➤ Zoom In, and View ➤ Zoom Out.

VIEW ➤ CUSTOM <PERCENTAGE>%

This command reduces or enlarges the display size of worksheet cells on the screen to a predetermined percentage of full size (100 percent).

To Zoom to a Custom View

1. Set your preferred default percentage of enlargement or reduction in View ➤ Set View Preferences ➤ Custom Zoom %.

2. From the View pull-down menu, select Custom <percentage>%.

VIEW ➤ ZOOM IN

 This command increases the display size of cells. Each time you select Zoom In, the display increases by 10 percent. You can set the display size of cells to as much as 400 percent.

To Zoom In

• From the View pull-down menu, select Zoom In.

 NOTES Use View ➤ Set View Preferences ➤ Custom Zoom % to reset cells to the default display size (87 percent).

VIEW ➤ ZOOM OUT

 This command decreases the display size of cells. Each time you select Zoom Out, the display decreases by 10% to as small as 25% of the normal size.

To Zoom Out

• From the View pull-down menu, select Zoom Out.

👁 **SEE ALSO** *Viewing Preferences*

Part III

@Function Reference

@Functions calculate formulas or perform algorithms using data values you specify in formula syntax as *arguments*. Each @function has its own syntax, typically one of the two shown below:

> **@FunctionName** by itself, with no arguments
>
> *or*
>
> **@FunctionName(Argument1,Argument2,...,ArgumentX)**

Parentheses, where shown, are mandatory in @function syntax. An @function and its arguments cannot exceed 512 characters in any single worksheet cell.

Arguments can be separated by commas (,) or semicolons (;). However, if you enter semicolons, the program will translate them to commas.

Some arguments require special words, or *keywords,* to set certain options or switches. Keywords and literal text values that are used as arguments must be enclosed in quotation marks (" "). Keywords are shown in this listing in all capital letters: SHEETNAME, for example.

Some of the optional arguments are binary switches, requiring a value of 0 or 1. In most cases, the 0 value can be omitted because it is the default setting.

Entries in this section give @function names, followed by argument syntax and definitions. Optional arguments, which can be omitted, are enclosed in brackets ([]).

For a list and explanations of arguments commonly used in 1-2-3 @functions, turn the page.

COMMONLY USED ARGUMENTS

Commonly used arguments in @functions include the following:

Basis   Is an optional day-count basis: 0 (0/360-day year), 1 (actual; default), 2 (actual/360), or 3 (actual/365).

Coupon   Is the annual rate of a coupon for a security.

Date-Number   Is a serial date number (usually 1900 date system).

Day-Of-Month   Can be 0 (same as Start-Date), 1 (first day of Month), or 2 (last day).

Direction   Of approximation in mathematical functions can be up (1), to the nearest multiple (0), or down (–1).

First-Interest   Is the first date on which interest will be paid.

Frequency   Of payments can be: 1 (annual), 2 (semiannual; default if omitted), 4 (quarterly), or 12 (monthly).

Guess   Must be a decimal 0–1, representing 0–100 percent estimated rate of return.

Holidays-Range   A range containing serial date values to specify holidays to exclude.

Issue   Is the date of issue of a certificate, bond, or other security.

Par   On an investment is the amount of the principal at maturity.

Settlement   On an investment is the call or settlement date.

Type   Is the kind of annuity payment. For financial @functions, use 0 for ordinary annuities and 1 for an annuity payment due at the beginning of a payment period. For statistical @functions, see the individual entries below.

Weekends   An argument that is a string of digits 0–6, each specifying a day of the week to count as a weekend day. If omitted, the default is 56, indicating Saturday and Sunday. A sole digit of 7 used for this argument means there are no weekend days.

CALENDAR @FUNCTIONS

Calendar @functions calculate dates and times based on either arguments you specify or the current value in your computer system's clock/calendar.

Date and time values you use as arguments must be integers or cell addresses/names that contain integers. Dates and times entered as text strings, where permitted, must be in one of the valid 1-2-3 number formats for calendar data.

@d360(*Start-Date,End-Date***)**   Based on a 360-day year, calculates the interval between two date numbers (see *@date*).

@date(*Year,Month,Day***)**   Calculates the date number (value from 1–73050, representing 1/1/1900–12/31/2099) for the calendar date.

@datedif(*Start-Date,End-Date,Format*)   Calculates the number of years, months, or days between two date numbers.

@dateinfo(*Date-Number,Attribute*)   Returns information about a Date-Number.

@datestring(*Date-Number***)**   Converts a serial Date-Number to a label in International Date format.

@datevalue(*Text***)**   Converts a date expressed as a Text string into a date number (see *@date*).

@day(*Date-Number***)**   Extracts from a serial Date-Number only the day of the month (an integer from 1–31).

@days(*Start-Date,End-Date,[Basis]*)   Calculates the number of days between two dates.

@days360(*Start-Date,End-Date***)**   Similar to @d360, but uses a standard set by the Securities Industry Association.

@hour(*Time-Number***)**   Extracts from a Time-Number (see *@now, @time, @timevalue*) only the hour of the 24-hour day (0–23).

@minute(*Time-Number***)**   Extracts from a Time-Number (see *@time*) only the minutes value (0–59).

@month(*Date-Number***)**   Extracts from a Date-Number (see *@date*) only the month of the year (1–12).

@networkdays(*Start-Date,End-Date,[Holidays-Range],[Week-ends]***)** Returns the number of workdays between the Start-Date and the End-Date. The optional arguments Holidays-Range and Weekends are used to specify excluded days (see *Commonly Used Arguments*, above).

@nextmonth(*Start-Date,Months,[Day-of-Month],[Basis]***)** Returns the serial date number for the Day-of-Month that is a specified number of Months from Start-Date.

@now Converts the value in your computer's clock/calendar to a date number (see *@date*) and a time number (see *@time*).

@second(*Time-Number***)** Extracts from a Time-Number (see *@time*) only the seconds value (0–59).

@time(*Hour,Minutes,Seconds***)** Converts the time arguments to a time number (0–0.99988, representing 12:00:00AM–11:59:59PM).

@timevalue(*Text***)** Converts a time expressed as a Text string into a time number (see *@time*).

@today Converts the value in your computer's clock/calendar to a date number (see *@date*).

@weekday(*Date-Number***)** Extracts the day of the week from a Date-Number and displays it as an integer from 0 (Monday) through 6 (Sunday).

@workday(*Start-Date,Days,[Holidays-Range],[Weekends]***)** Calculates the date number that corresponds to the date that is a specified number of Days before or after Start-Date. The optional arguments Holidays-Range and Weekends are used to specify excluded days (see *Commonly Used Arguments*, above).

@year(*Date-Number***)** Extracts from a Date-Number (see *@date*) only the year (0–199, representing 1900–2099).

DATABASE @FUNCTIONS

Database @functions perform queries and statistical analyses in database tables in worksheets and external database systems.

In 1-2-3, a *database table* is a range that contains one column for each field of a typical database record, ordered from left to right in the order the fields appear in the records. The top row in the table contains column-heading labels that are used as field names. Column widths correspond to field lengths, and cell formatting controls data typing.

All database @functions except @dquery have the following syntax:

@*Function Name***(Input,Field,[Criteria])**

where

- *Input* is the location of the database table (range address or name).

- *Field* is the name, offset number, or cell address of the field in the table to be searched.

- *Criteria* can be a formula that performs a logical test to determine which records will be selected *or* the range address/name of a separate criteria range (which contains such formulas) *or* the range address/name of selected records. If you specify only one table as Input, you can omit the Criteria argument, and the @function will use all values in the table.

Example: **@davg(A5..G20,4,J4..J5)**

The database @functions and their syntax include the following:

@davg(*Input,Field,[Criteria]***)**   Determines the average of data values in the Field in the table located at Input that meet the Criteria range.

@dcount(*Input,Field,[Criteria]***)**   Counts all cells in the Field in the table located at Input that contain data, including labels but excluding blank cells, and optionally those that meet the Criteria.

@dget(*Input,Field,[Criteria]***)**   Searches the Field in the table located at Input and retrieves a data item (value or label) that meets the Criteria.

@dmax(*Input,Field,[Criteria]***)**   Retrieves the greatest value that meets the Criteria in the Field in the table located at Input.

@dmin(*Input,Field,[Criteria]*) Retrieves the least value that meets the Criteria in the Field.

@dpurecount(*Input,Field,Criteria*) Counts nonblank entries, excluding labels, in the Field in the table located at Input that meet the Criteria. (See *@dcount*.)

@dquery(*Function,[Ext-Arguments]*) Lets you use a data query Function—possibly with Ext-Arguments (external arguments)—of an external database system and places its result in a criteria range. Consult the database system's documentation for required Ext-Arguments and use valid argument separators, such as commas, in multiple arguments.

@dstd(*Input,Field,[Criteria]*) In the table located at Input, calculates the *population* standard deviation of values in a list, or Field, that meets the Criteria. *Standard deviation* is the degree to which values in a list vary from the mean. The population standard deviation tests all values in the list.

@dstds(*Input,Field,[Criteria]*) Same as @dstd, but calculates the *sample* standard deviation. The sample standard deviation tests only a portion, or sample, of items in a long list.

@dsum(*Input,Field,[Criteria]*) In the Field in the table located at Input, returns the sum of all values that meet the Criteria.

@dvar(*Input,Field,[Criteria]*) Determines the *population* variance of values that meet the Criteria in a Field in the table located at Input. Variance is the degree to which values in a list vary from the mean. The population variation tests all values in the list.

@dvars(*Input,Field,[Criteria]*) Same as @dvar, except determines the *sample* variance, based on a portion, or sample, of a long list.

ENGINEERING @FUNCTIONS

Engineering @functions provide engineering calculations and advanced mathematical operations, and convert numbers to hexadecimal and decimal formats. Bessel functions, which are required in some differential calculus equations, can be generated by some of these @functions for purposes of describing curves such as cylindrical symmetry, wave propagation, fluid motion, elasticity, and diffusion.

@besseli(*X,n*) Calculates the modified Bessel function of integer order $In(X)$. X can be any value with which to evaluate the function. The argument n is a positive integer.

@besselj(*X,n*) Calculates the Bessel function of integer order $Jn(X)$. X can be any value with which to evaluate the function. The argument n is a positive integer.

@besselk(*X,n*) Calculates the modified Bessel function of integer order $Kn(X)$. X can be any value with which to evaluate the function. The argument n is a positive integer.

@bessely(*X,n*) Calculates the Bessel function of integer order $Yn(x)$. X can be any value with which to evaluate the function. The argument n is a positive integer.

@beta(*Z,W*) Calculates the beta function of values Z and W.

@betai(*A,B,X*) Returns the incomplete beta function of value X based on values A and B.

@decimal(*Hexadecimal*) Converts a hexadecimal (base-16) number to a signed decimal.

@erf(*Lower-Limit,[Upper-Limit]*) Calculates the error function integrated between Lower-Limit and either zero or Upper-Limit.

@erfc(*X*) Calculates the complementary error function, integrated between X and *infinity* (∞).

@erfd(*X*) Calculates the derivative of the error function.

@gamma(*X*)   Calculates the gamma function, where *X* is any value except 0 and negative integers.

@gammai(*A,X,[Complement]*)   Calculates the incomplete gamma function.

@gammaln(*X*)   Calculates the natural logarithm of the gamma function.

@hex(*X*)   Converts a decimal number *X* to hexadecimal (base-16) notation.

@seriessum(*X,X,M,Coefficients*)   Calculates the sum of a power series.

FINANCIAL @FUNCTIONS

Financial @functions apply formulas for investment analysis, including capital budgeting, ordinary annuities, and single-sum compound interest. Interest values used as arguments must not equal zero and must be greater than −1. Arguments can be numeric values or cell addresses/names.

@accrued(*Settlement,Issue,First-Interest,Coupon,[Par],[Frequency],[Basis]*)   Calculates the accrued interest for bonds with periodic interest payments.

@cterm(*Interest,Future-Value,Present-Value*)   Calculates the *term*, or number of compounding periods, during which an investment will grow, assuming a fixed rate of Interest.

@db(*Cost,Salvage,Life,Period*)   Using the fixed declining balance method, calculates the depreciation allowance for an asset (Cost >= Salvage, Life > 2, Period >= 1).

@ddb(*Cost,Salvage,Life,Period*)   Using the double-declining balance method, calculates the depreciation allowance for an asset (*Cost >= Salvage, Life > 2, Period >= 1*).

@duration(*Settlement,Maturity,Coupon,Yield,[Frequency],[Basis]*)   Returns the annual duration of an investment in a bond.

@fv(*Payments,Interest,Term*)   Calculates an investment's future value, based on Payments of equal amounts.

@fval(*Payments,Interest,Term,[Type],[Present-Value]***)**   Calculates an investment's future value with a specified Present-Value, based on a series of equal Payments, earning a periodic Interest rate, over the number of payment periods in Term.

@ipaymt(*Principal,Interest,Term,Start-Period,[End-Period],[Type],[Future-Value]***)**   Calculates the cumulative interest portion of the periodic payment on the Principal at a given Interest rate for the Term of the loan.

@irate(*Term,Payment,Present-Value,[Type],[Future-Value],[Guess]***)**   Calculates the periodic interest rate necessary for an annuity (Present-Value) to grow to a Future-Value over the number of compounding periods (Term).

@irr(*Guess,Range***)**   Calculates the internal rate of return of proceeds from cash flow in Range.

@mduration(*Settlement,Maturity,Coupon,Yield,[Frequency],[Basis]***)**   Returns the modified annual duration of an investment in a bond.

@mirr(*Range,Finance-Rate,Reinvest-Rate,[Type]***)**   Calculates the modified internal rate of return profit for a series of cash-flow values generated by an investment.

@nper(*Payments,Interest,Future-Value,[Type],[Present-Value]***)**   Calculates the number of periods required for an annuity of a specified Present-Value to grow to a Future-Value based on an Interest rate.

@npv(*Interest,Range,[Type]***)**   Calculates the net present value (a discount for the time value of money) of a future series of values (Range) by a fixed rate of Interest. Helps control the timing of cash flows.

@paymt(*Principal,Interest,Term,[Type],[Future-Value]***)**   For an ordinary annuity or one that is due, calculates the loan payment based on the Interest and the number of payment periods over the Term of the loan.

@pmt(*Principal,Interest,Term***)**   Calculates the required payment amount for a loan.

@pmtc(*Principal,Interest,Term***)**   Use this instead of @pmt for Canadian loans.

@ppaymt(*Principal,Interest,Term,Start-Period,[End-Period],[Type],[Future-Value]***)**   Calculates the portion of each payment applied to repay the Principal on a loan at a given Interest rate for a specified number of payment periods (Term).

@price(*Settlement,Maturity,Coupon,Yield,[Redemption],[Frequency],[Basis]***)** Calculates the price per $100 face value for securities that pay periodic interest.

@pv(*Payments,Interest,Term***)** Calculates an investment's present value, based on Payments of equal amounts.

@pval(*Payments,Interest,Term,[Type],[Future- Value]***)** Calculates the present value of an investment with a specified Future-Value, based on an annuity, discounted at a periodic Interest rate over the Term.

@rate(*Future-Value,Present-Value,Term***)** Calculates the required rate of fixed interest that yields a desired Future-Value of an investment, compounded over the specified Term.

@sln(*Cost,Salvage,Life***)** Calculates the allowance for straight-line depreciation of an asset.

@syd(*Cost,Salvage,Life,Period***)** Using the sum-of-the-years'-digits method, calculates the depreciation allowance for an asset (Cost >= Salvage, Life >= 1, Period >= 1).

@term(*Payments,Interest,Future-Value***)** Calculates the investment term required to reach a desired Future-Value, based on Payments of equal amounts at a periodic Interest rate.

@vdb(*Cost,Salvage,Life,Start-Period,End-Period,[Depreciation-Factor],[Switch]***)** Using the variable-rate declining balance method, calculates the depreciation allowance for an asset (Cost > Salvage; Life > 0; Start-Period < End-Period, both decimals for fractions of years). If Switch = 0, the program switches automatically to straight-line depreciation if the result is greater than would be produced by the declining-balance method. If Switch = 1, the program never uses straight-line.

@yield(*Settlement,Maturity,Coupon,Price,[Redemption],[Frequency],[Basis]***)** Returns the yield for bonds and securities that pay periodic interest.

INFORMATION @FUNCTIONS

Information @functions report on the contents of cells, ranges, Solver, Version Manager, the operating system and the location where data is incomplete or missing in a worksheet.

@cell(*Attribute,Location***)**   Reports on the attributes of the first cell in the specified range address/name (Location). The Attribute argument must be one of the following keywords, enclosed in quotation marks:

ACROSS	LEFTBORDERCOLOR
ADDRESS	ORIENTATION
BACKGROUNDCOLOR	PARENTHESES
BOLD	PATTERN
BOTTOMBORDER	PATTERNCOLOR
BOTTOMBORDER-COLOR	PREFIX
COL	PROTECT
COLOR	RIGHTBORDER
CONTENTS	RIGHTBORDERCOLOR
COORD	ROTATION
DATATYPE	ROW
FILEDATE	SHEET
FILENAME	SHEETNAME
FONTFACE	TEXTCOLOR
FONTSIZE	TOPBORDER
FORMAT	TOPBORDERCOLOR

FORMULATYPE	TYPE
HALIGN	UNDERLINE
HEIGHT	VALIGN
ITALIC	WIDTH
LEFTBORDER	WRAP

@cellpointer(*Attribute*)   Reports on the attributes (see *@cell*) of the current cell (pointer location). (See the Attribute list under *@cell*.)

@cols(*Range*)   Counts the number of columns in Range.

@coord(*Worksheet,Column,Row,Absolute*)   Generates a cell address/name from the Worksheet number, Column number (convert letters to numbers), and Row number. The Absolute (1–8) argument determines variations of absolute, mixed, or relative references.

@err   Generates the value ERR (error condition). (See the Logical entry *@iserr*.)

@info(*Report-Code*)   Reports on program status according to the Report-Code, a keyword, which must be enclosed in quotation marks:

AUTHOR	OSRETURNCODE
CREATION-DATE	OSVERSION
DBRETURNCODE	RECALC
DBDRIVERMESSAGE	RELEASE
DBRECORDCOUNT	SETUP-USER-NAME
DIRECTORY	SCREEN-HEIGHT
EDITING-TIME	SCREEN-WIDTH
LAST-REVISION-BY	SELECTION
LAST-REVISION-DATE	SELECTION-PART
MACRO-STEP	SELECTION-TYPE
MACRO-TRACE	SYSTEM

MEMAVAIL	TOTMEM
MODE	WINDIR
NUMFILE	WORKSHEET-NUMBER
ORIGIN	WORKSHEET-SIZE

@na   Generates the value NA (not available).

@rangename(*Cell***)**   Returns the name of the range in which Cell is located.

@refconvert(*Reference***)**   Converts the 1-2-3 Reference—expressed as A1 column or worksheet letters A through IV—to numbers from 1 through 256. Also converts column or worksheet R1C1 numbers from 1 through 256 to their corresponding column or worksheet letters. (A1 is the default notation scheme; R1C1 notation identifies cells by row and column number.)

@rows(*Range***)**   Counts the number of rows in Range.

@scenarioinfo(*Option,Name,[Contributor]***)**   Returns information about a scenario (Name).

@scenariolast(*File-Name***)**   Returns the name of the most recently displayed scenario in a File-Name during the current 1-2-3 session.

@sheets(*Range***)**   Counts the number of worksheets in Range.

@solver(*Status-Code***)**   Reports on the status of the Solver program according to any one of the following Status-Code keywords: CONSISTENT, DONE, MOREANSWERS, NEEDGUESS, NUMANSWERS, OPTIMAL, PROGRESS, or RESULT.

@user   Is not available in Release 5. You can retrieve the user name with the formula @info("SETUP-USER-NAME").

@versioncurrent(*Range***)**   Returns the name of the current version in range.

@versiondata(*Option,Cell,Version-Range,Name,[Contributor]***)**   Returns the contents of a specified cell in a version (Name).

@versioninfo(*Option,Version-Range,Name,[Contributor]***)**   Returns information about a version (Name).

LOGICAL @FUNCTIONS

Logical @functions perform *Boolean* comparisons of values, or true-false tests, and return the result as either True (1) or False (0).

@false   Generates the value 0.

@if(*Condition,First-Result,Second-Result***)**   Performs a logical test Condition, such as X > Y. If true, First-Result is returned; if false, Second-Result is returned. First-Result and Second-Result can be formulas, values, strings, or the cell addresses/names that contain them. Enclose strings in quotation marks (" ").

@isaaf(*Function-Name***)**   Tests for Function-Name as the valid name of an add-in @function. Enclose the text string you specify for Function-Name in quotation marks (" ") and omit the @ symbol.

@isapp(*Application-Name***)**   Checks whether the add-in program Application-Name has been loaded into memory with the command Tools ➤ Add-In ➤ Load. Enclose the text string you specify for Application-Name in quotation marks (" ") and omit any file extension.

@iserr(*X***)**   Tests whether the current value of X is ERR (error condition). X can be a formula (specified by its address or cell name), data value, cell address/name, text string, or condition statement (X>Y).

@isfile(*File-Name,[Type]***)**   Tests whether File-Name resides in memory or on disk. Returns 1 (true), if found, or 0 (false) if not found.

@ismacro(*Name***)**   Tests whether Name is a defined add-in macro command. Returns 1 (true) if found, or 0 (false) if not found.

@isna(*X***)**   Tests whether the current value of X is NA (not available). X can be a formula (specified by its address or cell name), data value, cell address/name, text string, or condition statement (X>Y).

@isnumber(*X*)   Tests whether the current value of *X* is a data value, ERR (error condition), NA (not available), or blank. The result is false if *X* is a formula or label. *X* can be a formula (specified by its address or cell name), data value, cell address/name, text string, or condition statement (X>Y).

@isrange(*Range*)   Tests whether Range (address or name) is defined as a valid range in the worksheet.

@isstring(*X*)   Tests whether the current value of *X* is text or a label. The result is false if *X* is a data value, ERR (error condition), NA (not available), or blank. *X* can be a formula (specified by its address or cell name), data value, cell address/name, text string, or condition statement (X>Y).

@true   Generates the value 1.

LOOKUP @FUNCTIONS

Lookup @functions find the contents of a cell or range under conditions that you specify.

@@(*Location*)   Reports the contents of a cell address/name (Location), which can also be a formula that generates a cell address/name.

@choose(*X,List*)   Retrieves the *X*th item in a List—a range that holds a group of items with argument separators.

@hlookup(*X,Range,Row-Offset*)   Returns the nearest-match contents (based on *X*) of a cell at a specified Row-Offset of a horizontal (rowwise) lookup table Range. Depending on the data type in the first column of the table, *X* can be either a value or a string (enclosed in quotation marks).

@index(*Range,Column,Row,*[*Sheet*])   Reports the contents of the cell specified by the Range address/name and offsets for Column, Row, and (optionally) Sheet. (Convert column letters to numbers, offset by the starting column.)

@match(*Cell-Contents,Range,*[*Type*])   Reports the position of the cell in range whose contents match Cell-Contents.

@maxlookup(*Range-List*)   Returns an absolute cell or range reference, including the file name, to the cell that contains the greatest value in a list of ranges (Range-List).

@minlookup(*Range-List*)   Returns an absolute cell or range reference, including the file name, to the cell that contains the least value in a list of ranges (Range-List).

@vlookup(*X,Range,Column-Offset*)   Returns the nearest-match contents (based on *X*) of a cell at a specified Column-Offset of a vertical (columnwise) lookup table Range. Depending on the data type in the first row of the table, can be either a value or a string (enclosed in quotation marks).

@xindex(*Range,Column-Heading,Row-Heading,[Worksheet-Heading]*)   Returns a cell's contents at the intersection specified by Column-Heading, Row-Heading, and (optionally) Worksheet-Heading.

MATHEMATICAL @FUNCTIONS

Mathematical @functions perform arithmetic operations or mathematical functions on numeric values. Arguments can be numbers or cell addresses/names that contain numbers. In general, trigonometric functions require angle values expressed in radians. (To convert degrees to radians, multiply by @pi and divide by 180.)

@abs(*X*)   Returns the absolute value (a positive number) of *X*.

@acos(*X*)   Calculates the *arc cosine* (in radians), or inverse cosine, of the cosine of an angle.

@acosh(*X*)   Calculates the inverse hyperbolic cosine of an angle.

@acot(*X*)   Calculates the inverse cotangent x of an angle *X*, given in radians, between 0 and 180 degrees.

@acoth(*X*)   Calculates the inverse hyperbolic cotangent using the hyperbolic cotangent *X* of an angle.

@acsc(X)   Calculates the inverse cosecant x of an angle. Given in radians, from $-\pi/2$ through $\pi/2$ which represents an angle between –90 and 90 degrees.

@acsch(X)   Calculates the inverse hyperbolic cosecant using the hyperbolic cosecant X of an angle.

@asec(X)   Calculates the inverse secant X of an angle. X must be given in radians, from 0 through π, which represents an angle between 0 and 180 degrees.

@asech(X)   Calculates the inverse hyperbolic secant X of an angle.

@asin(X)   Calculates the arc hyperbolic sine (in radians), or inverse hyperbolic sine, of the sine X of an angle.

@asinh(X)   Calculates the arc sine (in radians), or inverse sine, of the hyperbolic sine X of an angle.

@atan(X)   Calculates the arc tangent (in radians), or inverse tangent, of the tangent X.

@atan2(X,Y)   Calculates the arc tangent (in radians), or inverse tangent, of the tangent Y/X of an angle. Y and X are the lengths of any two sides of a triangle ($X <> 0$).

@atanh(X)   Calculates the inverse hyperbolic tangent using the hyperbolic tangent X of an angle.

@cos(X)   Calculates the cosine of an angle X that is expressed in radians.

@cosh(X)   Calculates the hyperbolic cosine of X whose value is greater than or equal to 1.

@cot(X)   Calculates the *cotangent* of angle X. The cotangent is the ratio of the side adjacent an acute angle of a right triangle to the opposite side.

@coth(X)   Calculates the hyperbolic cotangent of X.

@csc(X)   Calculates the *cosecant* of angle X. The cosecant is the reciprocal of the sine.

@csch(X)   Calculates the hyperbolic cosecant of angle X, which is the reciprocal of the hyperbolic sine.

@degtorad(*Degrees*)   Converts degrees to radians.

@even(X)   Rounds the value X to the nearest even integer.

@exp(X)   Raises the constant *e* to the power *X* (*e*≅A=2.718282, −11355.1371 < *X* < 11356.5234).

@exp2(X)   Calculates the value of the constant *e* (approximately 2.718282) raised to the power (-*x*^2).

@fact(X)   Calculates the factorial of *X*.

@factln(X)   Calculates the natural logarithm of the factorial of *X*.

@int(X)   Returns the integer (whole-number) component of *X*.

@*large(Range,N)* Returns the *N*th largest value in Range.

@ln(X)   Calculates the natural logarithm (base *e*) of *X*.

@log(X)   Calculates the common logarithm (base 10) of *X*.

@MOD(X,Y)   Calculates the *modulus*, or remainder, of dividing *X* by *Y* (*X* <> 0).

@odd(X)   Rounds the value *X* away from 0 to the nearest odd integer.

@quotient(X,Y)   Calculates the result of $^{X}/_{Y}$, truncated to an integer.

@pi   Generates the constant (π), or the ratio of a circle's circumference to its diameter (π ≅A=3.14159).

@radtodeg(*Radians*)   Converts Radians to degrees.

@rand   Generates a random decimal value from 0–1, calculated to 17 decimal places.

@round(X,N)   Rounds the number *X* to the nearest coefficient (multiple) of the *N* of 10 (−100 < power *N* < 100).

@rounddown(X,[N],[Direction])   Rounds the value *X* down to the nearest multiple of the power of 10 specified by *N*.

@roundm(X,Multiple,[Direction])   Rounds *X* to the nearest Multiple.

@roundup(X,[N],[Direction])   Rounds the value *X* up to the nearest multiple of the power of 10 specified by *N*.

@sec(X)   Calculates the secant of angle *X*.

@sech(X)   Calculates the *hyperbolic secant* of angle *X*. The hyperbolic secant is the reciprocal of the hyperbolic cosine. The result of @sech is a value greater than 0 or less than or equal to 1.

@sign(*X*)   Checks for a signed number. If *X* is a positive value, the result = 1, a 0 value = 0, and a negative value = −1.

@sin(*X*)   Calculates the sine of an angle *X* that is expressed in radians.

@sinh(*X*)   Calculates the hyperbolic sine of angle *X*.

@small(*Range,N*)   Finds the *N*th smallest value in Range.

@sqrt(*X*)   Calculates the positive square root of a positive value *X*.

@sqrtpi(*X*)   Calculates the square root of $X^*\pi$.

@subtotal(*List*)   Adds the values in List. Use @subtotal to indicate which cells @grandtotal should sum.

@sum(*List*)   Returns the sum, or total, of values in the List.

@sumnegative(*List*)   Totals only the negative values in its List of arguments.

@sumpositive(*List*)   Totals only the positive values in its List of arguments.

@sumproduct(*List*)   For each position in a List of matched ranges (range references with argument separators), first multiplies the values, then calculates their sum.

@sumsq(*List*)   Calculates the sum of the squares of the values in List.

@sumxmy2(*Range1,Range2*)   Subtracts the values in Range2 from the corresponding cells in Range1, squares the differences, and then sums the results.

@tan(*X*)   Calculates the tangent of an angle *X* that is expressed in radians.

@tanh(*X*)   Calculates the *hyperbolic tangent* of angle *X*. The hyperbolic tangent is the sine divided by the cosine. Limits are -1<*result*<1.

@trunc(*X,[N]*)   Truncates *X* to *N* decimal places.

STATISTICAL @FUNCTIONS

Statistical @functions analyze and compile statistics about items in lists. Wherever the argument List is required, a range address/name containing a list may be used. A list, whether included in the argument itself or in a specified range, contains a series of values with argument separators or in separate cells.

@avedev(*List*)   From the values in List, calculates the average of the absolute deviations.

@avg(*List*)   Calculates the average of values in the List.

@binomial(*Trials,Successes,Probability,[Type]*)   Calculates the binomial probability mass function, also called the cumulative binomial distribution. The optional argument Type determines whether the result is exactly (0), at most (1), or at least (2) the probable number (Probability) of Successes.

@chidist(*X,Degrees-Freedom,[Type]*)   Calculates the chi-square distribution. If Type = 0, X will be the upper bound or critical value >= 0. If Type = 1, X is a significance level from 0–1.

@chitest(*Range1,[Range2]*)   Calculates a chi-square test for independence on the data in Range1, or a chi-square test for goodness of fit on the data in Range1 and Range2.

@combin(*N,R*)   Calculates the *binomial coefficient* for N and R. The binomial coefficient is the number of ways that R can be selected from N, without regard for order.

@correl(*Range1,Range2*)   Calculates the correlation coefficient of values in Range1 and Range2.

@count(*List*)   Counts the number of nonblank cells in the ranges listed in List (a series of range references with argument separators).

@cov(*Range1,Range2,[Type]*)   Calculates either the population or sample covariance of the values in Range1 and Range2. Type is population covariance (0) or sample covariance (1).

@critbinomial(*Trials,Probability,Alpha*)   Returns the largest integer for which the cumulative binomial distribution is less than or equal to Alpha.

@devsq(*List***)** Calculates the sum of squared deviations of a List from their mean.

@fdist(*X,Degrees-Freedom1,Degrees-Freedom2,[Type]***)** Calculates the F-distribution. If Type = 0, the result is the critical or upper bound >= 0. If Type = 1, the result is a probability from 0–1.

@ftest(*Range1,Range2***)** Performs an F-test and returns the associated probability.

@geomean(*List***)** Calculates the geometric mean of a List.

@grandtotal(*List***)** Calculates the sum of all cells in List that contain @subtotal in their formulas.

@harmean(*List***)** Calculates the harmonic mean of a List.

@kurtosis(*Range,[Type]***)** Calculates the *kurtosis,* or measure of concentration of a distribution about a mean, of a Range. Type can be population (0) or sample (1).

@max(*List***)** Returns the maximum, or highest, value in the List.

@median(*List***)** Returns the median value in List.

@min(*List***)** Returns the minimum, or least, value in the List.

@normal(*X,[Mean],[Std],[Type]***)** Calculates the normal distribution function for X. Type can be cumulative distribution (0), inverse cumulative distribution (1), or probability density (2).

@percentile(*X,Range***)** Calculates the Xth sample percentile among the values in Range.

@permut(*N,R***)** Calculates the number of ordered sequences (permutations) of R objects that can be selected from a total of N objects.

@poisson(*X,Mean,[Cumulative]***)** Calculates the *Poisson distribution*, a probability density function.

@prank(*X,Range,[Places]***)** Ranks the percentile of X in a Range.

@product(*List***)** Multiplies the values in List.

@pureavg(*List***)** Calculates the average of a List of values, ignoring all cells that contain labels.

@purecount(*List***)** Counts the cells in a List of ranges, excluding cells that contain labels.

@puremax(*List*) Finds the largest value in List, ignoring cells that contain labels.

@puremin(*List*) Finds the smallest value in List, ignoring all cells that contain labels.

@purestd(*List*) Calculates the population standard deviation of the values in List, ignoring cells that contain labels.

@purestds(*List*) Calculates the sample standard deviation of the values in List, ignoring cells that contain labels.

@purevar(*List*) Calculates the population variance in a List of values, ignoring cells that contain labels.

@purevars(*List*) Calculates the sample population variance in a List of values, ignoring cells that contain labels.

@rank(*Item,Range,[Order]*) Returns the size or position of Item in Range in relation to the other values in Range. The argument Order can be descending (0) or ascending (1).

@regression(*X-Range,Y-Range,Attribute,[Compute]*) Performs multiple linear regression and returns the specified statistic (Attribute). The values of Attribute can be 1–5, 101–175, or 201–275. (See the Help pages or manual for details.) The Compute switch specifies whether to use 0 as the Y intercept (0) or a calculated Y intercept (1). This @function is an exception in that 1 (calculated Y) is the default, not 0.

@semean(*List*) Calculates the standard error of the sample mean for the values in List.

@skewness(*Range,[Type]*) Calculates the degree to which values in Range are skewed. Type can be population (0) or sample (1).

@std(*List*) Calculates the population standard deviation (see *@dstd*).

@stds(*List*) Calculates the sample standard deviation (see *@dstds*).

@tdist(*X,Degrees-Freedom,[Type],[Tails]*) Calculates the Student's t-distribution.

@ttest(*Range1,Range2,[Type],[Tails]*) Performs a Student's t-test on the data in Range1 and Range2 and returns the associated probability. Type can be homoscedastic (0), heteroscedastic (1), or paired (2). The Tails direction of the test can be one-tailed (1) or two-tailed (2). The default is Tails = 2.

@**var**(*List*)   Calculates the population standard variance (see *@dvar*).

@**vars**(*List*)   Calculates the sample standard variance (see *@dvars*).

@**weightavg**(*Data-Range,Weights-Range,[Type]*)   Calculates the weighted average of values in Data-Range. Type can be sum of values in Weights-Range (0) or number of values in Data-Range (1).

@**ztest**(*Range1,Mean1,Std1,[Tails],[Range2],[Mean2],[Std2]*)
Performs a z-test on one or two populations and returns a probability. For each range, Mean is the population mean and Std is the population standard deviation. The list can be any combination of ranges. The Tails direction of the test can be one-tailed (1) or two-tailed (2). The default is Tails = 2.

TEXT @FUNCTIONS

Text @functions apply transformations to text strings. LMBCS codes refer to the Lotus MultiByte Character Set. In general, strings can be string values enclosed in quotation marks, formulas that generate label values, or cell addresses/names that contain strings.

@**char**(*X*)   Returns the LMBCS equivalent of an integer *X*.

@**clean**(*Text*)   Removes nonprinting characters from Text.

@**code**(*Text*)   Returns the LMBCS code of the first character in a Text string.

@**exact**(*Text1,Text2*)   Compares two strings and returns True (1) if they match and False (0) if they differ.

@**find**(*Search-Text,Text,Start-Number*)   Searches for Text within a longer string (Search-Text), beginning at a specified character Start-Number (integer). Returns the character position of the first character in the matching string.

@**left**(*Text,N*)   Returns the first *N* characters in Text, counting from its left end.

@**length**(*Text*)   Counts the number of characters in Text.

@lower(*Text***)**   Converts all characters in Text to lowercase.

@mid(*Text,Start-Number,N***)**   Returns N consecutive characters from Text, beginning at the specified character Start-Number.

@n(*Range***)**   Returns the numeric value contained in the first cell in Range. If non-numeric, returns a value of 0.

@proper(*Text***)**   Makes the first character in Text a capital letter and the rest lowercase.

@repeat(*Text,X***)**   Duplicates the Text value X times.

@replace(*Original-Text,Start-Number,N,New-Text***)**   In Original-Text, starting at Start-Number character position counting from the left, replaces N characters with New-Text. If N = 0, the insertion is made without deleting any characters.

@right(*Text,N***)**   Returns the last N characters in Text, counting from its right end.

@s(*Range***)**   Returns the value in the first cell in Range as a label.

@setstring(*Text,Length,[Alignment]***)**   Aligns its Text argument within a specified number of blank spaces. Length in characters can be 0–512 (the maximum number of characters in a cell). Alignment of characters in cells can be 0 (left), 1 (center), or 2 (right).

@string(*X,N***)**   Converts a value X to a label formatted as specified by N: 0–116 (Fixed, N decimal places), 1000–1116 (Comma, N–1000 decimal places), –18–1 (Scientific, ABS(N) digits), 10001–10512 (General, up to N–10000 characters).

@trim(*Text***)**   Deletes unnecessary space characters from Text, including leading, trailing, and multiple internal consecutive spaces.

@upper(*Text***)**   Converts all characters to capitals, or uppercase.

@value(*Text***)**   Converts numeric digits that were entered as label data into a numeric value.

Index

Page numbers in **boldface** refer to primary entries.

Symbols & Numbers

$ (dollar sign), for absolute cell addresses, 183
& operator, for concatenation, 86
******* (asterisks), in place of numeric values, 45, 153
✓ button, 2
+ (plus sign), to begin formulas, 83
+/− number format, 153
{} (braces), for macro command, 129
, (Comma) number format, 153, 244
"" (quotation marks), for literal strings, 86
@ functions, **247–270**. *See also specific function names under first letter of function*
    calendar, **249–250**
    choosing and pasting, 10
    database, **250–252**
    engineering, **253–254**
    financial, **254–256**
    information, **257–259**
    logical, **260–261**
    lookup, **261–262**
    mathematical, **262–265**
    new to Release 5, 6
    statistical, **266–269**
    text, **269–270**
@@ function, 261
@Function List dialog box, 10
@Function Selector, **10–11**
1-2-3 database table, report generation from, **189–190**
1-2-3 file, as model for external database tables, 216
1-2-3 Pic file type, 156
1-2-3.WK* file type, 155
1-way analysis
    for cross tabulation, 237
    for sensitivity analysis, 236
2-way analysis
    for cross tabulation, 237
    for sensitivity analysis, 236
3D area charts, 35
3D bar charts, 35, 36
3D line charts, 35, 36
3D pie charts, 34, 36
3D range, inverting, 105
3D worksheets, 211
3-dimensional transposition, 221
3-way analysis
    for cross tabulation, 237
    for sensitivity analysis, 236
123R5.INI file, 225

A

About 1-2-3 (Help menu), 97
@abs function, 262
absolute cell addresses, 183
accelerator keys, 88, **107–110**, 125
@accrued function, 254
@acos function, 262
@acosh function, 262
@acot function, 262
@acoth function, 262
@acsc function, 263
@acsch function, 263
active windows, 242
add-ins, **12–13**
addressing, **13–14**. *See also* cell addresses
Adjustable Cells, in Solver, 206
.ADW file extension, 12
aggregating database queries, **14–16**
alias name, 146
alignment, **16–19**, 244
All files (*.*) file type, 156
Allow Updates to Database Table option, 180
Allways add-in program, 159

SmartIcons in 1-2-3

Spacer

Create a file

Create a plain new file
(New)

Open an existing file

Save the current file

Display the Print
dialog box

Print the current selection
(New)

Preview the print selection

Close the active window

End the 1-2-3 session

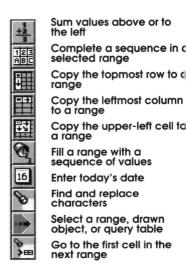

Sum values above or to
the left

Complete a sequence in a
selected range

Copy the topmost row to a
range

Copy the leftmost column
to a range

Copy the upper-left cell to
a range

Fill a range with a
sequence of values

Enter today's date

Find and replace
characters

Select a range, drawn
object, or query table

Go to the first cell in the
next range

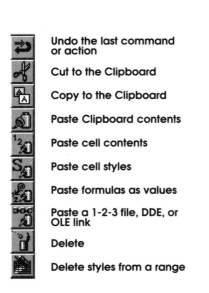

Undo the last command
or action

Cut to the Clipboard

Copy to the Clipboard

Paste Clipboard contents

Paste cell contents

Paste cell styles

Paste formulas as values

Paste a 1-2-3 file, DDE, or
OLE link

Delete

Delete styles from a range

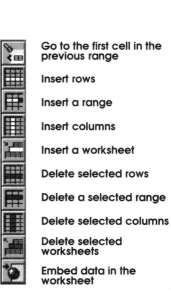

Go to the first cell in the
previous range

Insert rows

Insert a range

Insert columns

Insert a worksheet

Delete selected rows

Delete a selected range

Delete selected columns

Delete selected
worksheets

Embed data in the
worksheet